FEBRUARY 2022

AN ANTHOLOGY OF ARTICLES

BRAIN BOOSTER ARTICLES

Copyright © Brain Booster Articles
All Rights Reserved.

Contents

Preface

"Start writing, no matter what. The water does not flow until the faucet is turned on".

-Louis L'Amour

This book is a bouquet of articles contributed by students, professors and academicians. Hundreds of students and professors are contributing their work to Brain Booster Articles, we are here to provide ample information about Law and Contemporary issues. Our aim is to provide a platform for today's generation to express their views and ideas on law and contemporary law.

CHAPTER ONE

BRIEF ANALYSIS OF PRIVITY OF CONTRACT AND PRIVITY OF CONSIDERATION

Author: Aditi Vyas, II year of B.B.A.,LL.B. from BM Law College

Co-author: Vipul Solanki, II year of B.B.A.,LL.B. from BM Law College

Introduction

A contract has been defined as "an agreement enforceable by law"[i]. Also, the section 2(d) represents consideration, "When at the desire of the promisor, promisee or any other person has done or abstained from doing or does or abstains from doing or promises to do or to abstain from doing something, such act or abstinence, or promise is called a consideration for the promise." If a contract fulfilled by the promise in favour of any other person other than the parties to the contract the other person would be a "stranger to the contract." In English law, consideration must not move from the promise, which means a stranger to the consideration cannot sue. This is known as privity of consideration. The scenario for the same is different in India; a stranger to the consideration can also sue as defined under section 2(d) of the Indian contract act. The rule of privity of contract is equally applicable in India and England.

Privity of Consideration

The rule of Privity of consideration doesn't apply in India. When at the desire of the promisor, the promisee or any other person has done or abstained from doing, or does or abstains from doing, or promises to do or to abstain from doing, something, such act or abstinence or promise is called a consideration for the contract.[ii]The promisee or any other person may give consideration. In England, the position differs from India's; the consideration rule must move from the promisee to nobody else. Unlike India, consideration may move not from the promisee but a third person, who may not be a party to the contract.

To better understand the concept here's and example, A promises to sell his Mobile Phone to B and the consideration of Rs. 10,000 for the same is given to A by B's son X, who is not a party to the contract. This will not be a valid contract in England as the consideration for the phone was given by a third party and not the promise; meanwhile, in India, it will constitute a valid contract as under Section 2 (d) [iii]of The Indian Contract Act.

Furthermore, in a leading case of Chinmaya v. Ramayya[iv]: A, an old lady gifted her property to her daughter (defendant) by a gift deed with a consideration of her paying an annuity of Rs. 653 to A's brothers(plaintiffs). The defendant promised to fulfil the same to pay the grant to the plaintiffs. But, the defendant was unable to complete the consideration. In action against the defendant, she resisted that they had no right of action since the plaintiff had given no consideration. The Madras High Court held that the defendant's mother provided the review, which was enough to enforce the promise between the two parties.

In the above case law, it has been shown that the plaintiffs themselves did not give the consideration but a third party. According to the rule under Indian Law, a review can be provided either by the promisee or any other person. Meanwhile in England, the government is different. A stranger to a contract cannot enforce the agreement.[v]

<u>Privity of Contract</u>

Privity of contract is defined as "A contract cannot be enforced by a person who is not a party to it even though it is made for his benefit. He is a 'stranger to the contract' and can claim no right under it".[vi]

This ruleis also based on "interest theory", this theory says that a person having an interest in the agreement is entitled to sue as per the law to protect his rights.

The principle is generally applicable in India, and only a party to the contract can enforce the agreement or file a suit for the enforcement of the deal.

The principle of privity of contract can be distinguished from the privity of consideration; in the rule of privity of consideration, it has been stated that a person who has himself not given any consideration can take measures to enforce a contract if he is a party to the contract as consideration can be either provided by the promise or any other person.[vii]

The rule of privity of contract is equally applicable in Indian and English Law. The rule of privity of contract was based upon the law laid down in the case of Tweddle v. Atkinson in England, which was further developed[viii].

In the case of Tweddle v. Atkinson, A married to a girl B, after the marriage, there was a contract between the father of A and the father of B, that both of them would individually pay a certain amount to A. A will be able to sue each of them in case of non-fulfilment of the payment. After the death of both the father's a bought a suit against the executors of B's father for the sum of money. In the suit, it was held that A could not sue as he was a stranger to the contract and a stranger to consideration for the same.

After this case, there was another case of Dunlop Pneumatic Tyre Co Ltd. V. Selfridge & Co. Ltd.,[ix]in this case, Dunlop & Co. (appellants) was a manufacturer co. of tyres, they made a contract with Dew & co. for certain tyres, and in the contract, it was stated that dew and tyres must not sell any tyre below the given price list. Dew & Co. sold some of these tyres to Selfridge and Co.(respondents) with the condition of the price list being fulfilled and a penalty of 5 Euros for each tyre sold below the price list. Selfridge & Co. sold some tyres below the price list. In a suit bought by the appellants against the respondents, it was held that the respondent was not liable since they were strangers to the contract of the appellant and Dew & co. Along with that, respondents were also stranger to consideration in the contract made between the appellants and Dew & Co. Ltd.

<u>Position of privity of contract in India</u>

The rule of privity of contract is equally applicable in India as it is applicable in the case of England, given that the definition of consideration is extensive in the Indian Contract Act. This rule is applicable in India in almost every circumstance.

Let us explain this example further with a real-life incident, A mortgages his property to B in consideration of B's promise to Manis that he shall pay A's debt to X, X cannot file a suit against B to enforce his promise because X was not a party to the contract made between A and B.[x]

To better understand, let us look into a case law of Advertising Bureau v. C.T. Devaraj[xi], in which a circus owner made a deal with the financer who would make an advertisement for the circus. The advertiser(plaintiff) did not make any contract with the financer for the advertising of the circus.

Since the advertiser was a stranger to the contract and there was no contract between him and the financer, a suit brought against the financer by the advertiser, it was held that the suit was dismissed on the basis, there being no contract between the advertiser and financer and the advertiser being a third party to the contract between the circus owner and the financer.

<u>Exceptions to privity of contract</u>

1) Trust of contractual rights or beneficiary under the contract

Under this exception, a beneficiary of a trust can sue by enforcing his right under the trust in a contract made between a trustee of a trust and another party, even if the person suing is a stranger to the contract.

In Indian law, this exception is recognised in the case of Khwaja Muhammad khan v. Huasini Begum[xii]. In the suit brought, there existed an agreement between a father of a girl and the father of a boy that if the girl marries a particular boy, the defendant will pay certain personal allowances known as kharchi-i-pandan[xiii]. The contract also mentioned that certain property was kept aside by the defendant and the allowances had to be paid out of the income generated out of the property. The girl married the defendant's son but the defendant is unable to fulfil the personal allowances. In an action bought by the plaintiff, the defendant argued that the contract has been made with the plaintiff's father and not with the plaintiff, therefore, being a stranger to the contract she cannot sue. The argument made by the defendant was in reference to the case of Tweddle v. Atkinson[xiv]. It was held that the plaintiff was entitled to claim the same since she was a beneficiary to the contract.

In another case of KalusMittlebachert v. East India Hotels Ltd.,[xv] Klaus Mittlebachert was a pilot in the Lufthansa airlines, and her landed his flight in Delhi the owners of Lufthansa airlines had a contract with the Hotel Oberoi Inter-continental(defendants) that the crew members of the Lufthansa airlines will stay in the hotel for their lay over. In the hotel there was swimming pool which had a diving board. The plaintiff, one day went to the pool and used the diving board to dive into the pool got injuries as his head got an accident with floor of the pool. The plaintiff suffered serious injuries and was paralyzed, and after suffering for 13 years he died. In a suit brought against the hotel management the hotel was held liable. In defence, the hotel pleaded that the plaintiff was not a party to the contract and he could not sue. But it was held that the plaintiff was a beneficiary to the contract so he could sue and he succeeded.

2) Conduct, acknowledgement, or admission

Sometimes there may be no privity of contract between the two parties, but if one of them by his conduct, acknowledgement, or admission recognizes the right of the other to sue him, he may be liable on the basis of the law of estoppel.

This exception could be seen in the case of Narayani Devi vs. Tagore Commercial Corporation Ltd[xvi]. Here there was an agreement made between the plaintiff's husband and the defendants that the defendants need to pay a particular amount to the plaintiff's husband during his lifetime and thereafter to the plaintiff. After, the death of the plaintiff the defendants had made certain payments to the plaintiff but after sometime the defendant asked for extension of time to pay. Apart from that the defendants by their admission had call upon the plaintiff to execute some documents which implies that the plaintiff to be entitled to certain rights. It was held that the defendants had created the privity with the plaintiff by their conduct and acknowledgement that the plaintiff was entitled to her action even though there was no privity to contract between the defendants and the plaintiff

3) Marriage expenses or maintenance under family arrangements

In a family arrangement or a marriage if a contract is made to give a benefit to the third party he can sue to claim for the same as the beneficiary. Such actions are allowed in many cases on the partition of joint family property between the male members, a provision is made for the maintenance of the female members of the family. The rule laid down in the case of Khawaja Muhammad khan v. Huasini Begum[xvii] is the basis for the recognition of such an action.

In the case of Veeramma v. appayya[xviii], under a family agreement, the father's house was to be given to his daughter and the daughter undertook to maintain him in his lifetime. The daughter is a beneficiary under the arrangement it was held that she was entitled to sue for the specific performance in her favour.

CHAPTER TWO

CONCEPT OF BAIL: A HISTORICAL PERSPECTIVE

Author: Devansh Bansal, Pursuing LL.M. from Christ University

ABSTRACT

The concept of bail has a long history and deep roots in English and American law. In medieval England, the custom grew out of the need to free untried prisoners from disease-ridden jails while waiting for the delayed trials to be conducted by traveling justice. [1]Prisoners were bailed or delivered to reputable third parties of their choosing who accepted responsibility for assuring their appearance at trial. Suppose the accused did not appear; his bail would stand the test in his place. Eventually, it became the practice for property owners who accepted responsibility for accused persons to forfeit money when their charges failed to appear for trial. From this grew the modern practice of posting a money bond through a commercial bondsman who receives a cash premium for his service and usually demands some collateral. In the event of non-appearance, the bond is forfeited after a grace period of several days during which the bondsman may produce the accused in Court.[2] Usually, bail is a kind of asset or property given by the court as security for consideration of release from being arrested or to avoid being jailed, as an identification that the accused or suspect will be present on the day of hearing or trial and where if he fails to appear before the court on the given day then his property may be sized or forfeit the bail. The amount deposited shall be returned at the trial's end if the accused is present at every hearing, regardless of whether the accused has been found guilty oracquitted.

The administration of bail has seen changed enormously from this original bail setting. These changes in America can be attributed mainly to the intersection during the 20th century of two historical phenomena.

<u>INTRODUCTION</u>

The slow evolution from the personal surety system using unsecured financial conditions to a commercial one primarily using secured economicneeds. The second was the often misunderstood creation and nurturing of bail or no bail or release or no release dichotomy, which continues today.

The history of bail tells us that the pre-trial releases and detention system worked effectively over the centuries. Moreover, the bail side of the dichotomy functioned most effectively through an uncompensated and un-indemnified personal surety system based on unsecured financial conditions. What we in America today know as the traditional money bail system – a system relying primarily on secured economic conditions administered through commercial sureties is, historically speaking, a relatively new approach that was encouraged to solve America"s dilemma of the unnecessary detention of bailable defendants in the 1800s. Unfortunately, however, the traditional money bail system has only exacerbated the two primary cases of abuse that have typically led to historicalcorrection:

1. The unnecessary detention of bailable defendants, whom we now often categorize as lower risk.

2. The release of those we feel should be unbailable defendants and whom we now often categorize as higherrisk.

The history of bail also instructs us on the proper purpose of bail. Specifically, while avoiding blood feuds may have been the primary purpose for the original bail setting, once more public processes and jails were fully introduced into the administration of criminal justice, the purpose of bail changed to one of providing a mechanism of conditional release. Concomitantly, the purpose of, no bail was and is detention. Historically speaking, the only goal for limiting or conditioning pre-trial release was to assure that the accused come to court or otherwise face justice. That changed in the 1970s and 1980s, as jurisdictions began to recognize public safety as a second constitutionally valid.

The Purpose for limiting pre-trial freedom. It is a matter of court to grant bail or not in some countries, bail is commonly allowed, and in some countries, it is tough to get bail. If the courts find that the accused will not appear in court if he is permitted bail and there is a chance that he will abscond in such cases, the court may not let bail.

ORIGIN OF THE WORD BAIL

Bail is derived from the old French verb baillie, which means giving or delivering. The word is also related to the Latin word bajulare, meaning to bear a burden.[3] It allows individuals to live their lives until they are brought to trial, giving them a taste of freedom while preparing their defense. Bail itself has a fascinating history – and how it has been applied often says quite a bit about the relationship between the legal system and those who have been accused of a crime. Bail origins are ancient, but the concept has been familiar throughouthistory.[4]

While bail can be traced to ancient Rome, our traditional American understanding derives primarily from English roots. When the Germanic tribes, the Angles, the Saxons, and the Jutes migrated to Britain after the fall of Rome in the fifth century, they brought with them the blood feud asthe primary means of settling disputes. Whenever one person wronged another, the families of the accused and the victim would often pursue a private war until all persons in one or both of the families were killed. However, this form of „justice" was brutal and costly, so these tribes quickly settled on a different legal system based on compensation, first with goods and later with money to fix wrongs. This compensation, in turn, was based on the concept of the„ wergild, "meaning„ manprice" or „manpayment "and some times more generally called a „bot," which was a value placed on every person and appears on every person's property", according to social rank.

HISTORY OF BAIL UNDER INDIAN LAW

Historical genesis the ethos and injunctions of ancient Hindu jurisprudence required,among other things, suitable disposal of disputes by the functionaries responsible for the administration of justice. No laxity could be afforded in thematter as it entailed penalties on the functionaries.[5] Thus, a judicial interposition ensured that an accused person was not unnecessarily detained or incarcerated. This indeed devised practical modes both for securing the presence of a wrongdoer and spare him of undue strains on his freedom.[6]

During Moghul Rule

The Indian legal system is recorded to have an institution of bail to release an arrested person on his furnishing a surety. This system finds reference in the seventeenth-century travelogue of Italian traveler Manucci. [7]Manucci himself was restored to his freedom from imprisonment on a false theft charge. The then ruler of Punjab granted him bail, but Kotwal released him on bail only after Manucci furnished a surety. Under Moghul law, an interim release could be actuated by considering that if the dispensation of justice got delayed in one's case, compensatory claims could be made on the judge himself for losses sustained by the aggrievedparty.

The advent of British rule in India saw a gradual adaptation of the principles and practices known to Britishers and was prevalent in the common law. The East India Company"s total control over Nizamat Adalats and other Fouzdary Courts in the mofussil saw gradual inroads of English criminal law and procedure in the then Indian legal system.

BAIL UNDER THE CRIMINAL PROCEDURE CODE,1973

The word bail has not been defined in the Code of Criminal Procedure. However, the Codes of 1898 and 1973 have defined the expression „bailable offense" and „non-bailable offense, "respectively in Section 4(1)(b)[8]and Section 2(a).[9] In the latter section, the expression „bailable offense" has been defined to mean an offense which is shown as bailable in Schedule I, or which is made bailable by any other law for the time being in force, and the expression„ non-bailable" has been defined to mean any other offense.

MEANING OF BAIL

Bail is simply the process of releasing a person who may be on his bond or some security; bail is the post-arrest process and before trial. In the criminal procedure code, bail is not defined anywhere. Still, classification of offenses into bailable and non-bailableviolations made expressly or may be made after examining the gravity of crimes. Grave crimes to be made non-bailable, where bail not to be granted as a right but to be given on looking certain factors by exercising the judicial discretion by courts on some just and human grounds.7

CLASSIFICATION OF OFFENCES

Bailable Offence

A bailableoffense means an offensethat has been categorized as bailable. In case of such violation, bail can be claimed, subject to fulfillment of certain conditions, as a matter of right under Section 436 of The Criminal Procedure Code, 1973. In case of bailable offenses, the Police areauthorized to give bail to the accused at the time of arrest or detention. As defined under Section 2(a) of the code – a bailable offence means an offensethat is shown as bailable in theFirst Schedule, or which is made bailable by any other law for the time being in force; and non-bailable offence means any other offence.[10]

Non-bailable Offence

Non-bailable means an offense in which bail cannot be granted as a matter of right, except on the orders of a competent court. In such cases, the accused can apply for a grant of bail under Sections 437 and 439 of the code.[11] Grant of bail in a non-bailable offense is subject to the judicial discretion of the Court, and it has been mandated by the Supreme Court of India that "Bail, not Jail" should be the governing and guidingprinciple.

OBJECTS OF BAIL

It is not the object of the criminal law to confine a person accused of a crime before his conviction. Bail, in criminal cases, is, therefore, intended to combine the administration of justice with the liberty and convenience of the person alleged accused.

Administration of justice on the spot or immediately after the commission of a crime by the fundamental principles ofnatural justice embedded in a fair and just legal system is not feasible. This appears to be one of the reasons for the evolution of the bail jurisdiction in any legal system. The release on bail is crucial to the accused as pre-trial detention consequences are against the presumption of innocence. If release on bail is denied to the accused, it would mean that though he is presumed to be innocent till the guilt is proved beyond a reasonable doubt, he would be subjected to the psychological and physical deprivations of jail life. The jailed accused loses his job and is prevented from contributing effectively to defense preparation. Equally important, the burden of his detention frequently falls heavily on the innocent members of his family.

CONCLUSION

From the previously mentioned dialog plainly Bail matter assumes a critical part in a criminal case, since it is a definitive objective of the denounced. Bail is the privilege of the gathering. Anybody needs a bail who is captured living in prison implies they need a bail whenever. To set free, or convey from capture, or out of care, on the endeavor of some other individual or people that he or they will be in charge of the appearance, at a specific day and place, of the individual bailed. At the point when bail has been orchestrated, the blamed individual is permitted to go free until the trail. Be that as it may, in the event of non-bail capable offense, there is no particular arrangement in Cr.P.C of Bangladesh. The anguish of the general individuals will be diminished and the judges won't be one-sided by the power of the political party or controlling gathering to satisfy their need on the off chance that it is conceivable to embrace fitting arrangements in Bangladesh. So we ought to present particular arrangement of bail if there should arise an occurrence of non-bail capable offense. For instance, as indicated by segment 339(c) of the CrPC, a Magistrate can't go past the time scope of 180 days to close the trial and a Session Judge gets 360 days to finish up it. In the event that the trial isn't finished inside this time traverse, the blamed despite the fact that he is charged for non-bail capable offense, might be discharged on bail.

CHAPTER THREE

MARITAL RAPE IN INDIA

Author: Rahul Aaditya, IV year of B.CA.,LL.B.(Hons.) from SCHOOL OF EXCELLENCE IN LAW (SOEL)

Co-author: Sai Madhumita Saravanan, III year of B.Com.,LL.B.(Hons.) from SCHOOL OF EXCELLENCE IN LAW (SOEL)

ABSTRACT

Rape is a crime of utmost savagery against women so is marital rape. The concept of Marital rape is where the victim is forced to have sexual intercourse with his/her spouse. In simple words when the victim is raped by his/her own spouse it amounts to marital rape. But here in our country this brutal crime has not yet been categorized as a criminal offense but is deemed as a civil offense, under the Domestic Protection Act. It is treated as a criminal offense only if the victim is below the age of 18. This type of odious crime is still prevalent in many parts of India and the victim can seek a remedy under the Civil Act. The main objective of this paper is to outline the severity of Marital rape and not being punishable as a criminal offense under IPC for victims above the age of 18.

INTRODUCTION

Rape like all of us know is not only a crime of utmost savagery against women but also a violation of an individual's basic rights such as protection of life and personal liberty.

The Guwahati HC in the case of Nasiruddin Ali VS The State of Assam[i] held that rape is a violation of the fundamental rights of the victim under Article 21[ii] of the Constitution. The article guarantees an individual two rights namely, the Right to Life and the Right to Personal Liberty.

In India Rape is not seenas just another form of sexual abuse but as a very serious crime because of the patriarchal values imbibed in the society. There is a judgmental opinion by the society,on the woman if she loses her virginity before the marriage. There are high chances of her not getting married at all. If this is the case for matron women, then what would be the situation for Rape victims who had lost their Virginity without their consent? There have been numerous instances, where the Rape victim's family hascommitted suicide, just because they couldn't handle the pressure of society. But in contrast, the same society accepts Marital rape (Marital Rape or Spousal Rape in simple words is nothing but rape committed by the person to whom the victim is married) while it gets furious over Rape issues.

As of today, there are only seven countries in the world (UAE, Pakistan, China, Iran, Bangladesh, Saudi Arabia) where rape convicts are punished with the death penalty, and India is one among them. But in contrast in the year 2022, about 150 plus countries have criminalized Marital rape and only 32 countries in the world haven't criminalized it. Sadly, India is one of them. When activists and the public of India have raised their voice in the past to provide severe punishments for Rape, (similar to punishments given by countries that follow the deterrent theory of punishment) then why are the same public quiet about marital rape, does marriage amount to implied consent for sex?

<u>MARITAL IS NOT JUST ANOTHER FORM OF DOMESTIC VIOLENCE</u>

Domestic violence against women is one of the major issues in India which has been exacerbated in recent times. The NCRB (National Crime Records Bureau) reported that in the year 2019 about 70 percent of the female population in India fell prey to domestic violence of one sort or the other. But in 2020 the NCRB stated that the violence against women dropped by 8.3 percent when compared to 2019. The data exhibited by the National Commission of Women shows a different picture, stating that from the month of February to May alone the domestic cases filed increased by 2.5 times. Approximately 1500 domestic complaints were lodged during this period.

As all of us know marital rape is one such form of domestic violence. It may not be surprising if we regard marital rape just not as another form of Domestic violence but as a crime against the spouse's personal liberty.

The relationship between the victim and the perpetrator is in no way going to reduce the post psychological, emotional, and physical effects that rape is going to have on the victim. As a survivor of sexual assault, the wife is going to face depression, flashbacks (memories of past trauma appear as if they are taking place currently), and PTSD (post-traumatic stress disorder). The victims may indulge in self-harm, substance abuse (intake of drugs such as Cocaine and Marijuana), and even disassociation from their close ones as it's the most common form of defense mechanism that the brain uses to cope with traumas, especially traumas of sexual violence. The post effects of sexual assault may even have permanent effects on the victim, where the victim may suffer from a sleeping disorder, eating disorder, and sometimes even panic attacks.

Therefore, we shouldn't try to convince ourselves by stating that married couples are completely protected by the "Protection of Women from Domestic Violence Act 2005"as the offense is covered under this act. Yes, the term sexual abuse does come under one of those acts that amount to domestic violence, but this doesn't mean that this act is appropriate enough to deal with cases regarding Marital Rape. This act may define what sexual abuse is but it doesn't outweigh the severity of rape as stated under section 375 of the Indian Penal Code. Therefore, this law is just going to treat Marital rape as another form of sexual abuse and in turn, reduces the intensity of this crime. Also, the domestic violence act is deemed to come under civil law as well. Hence, there are possibilities where the accused can get away without even a jail sentence as he has committed only a civil wrong and not a criminal offense. When raping an unmarried woman is deemed to be a criminal offense under sec.375 of the IPC, then why should spouses who commit marital rape be given immunity for such a severe crime?

INDIAN LAWS ON MARITAL RAPE

Immunity Guaranteed by IPC for Marital Rape

The concept of Marital Rape in India is a legalized weapon for men to rape their wives. Rape is considered a criminal offense under sec.375 of the IPC. Under the sec. there are six conditions, which constitute rape, of which one of the conditions states that "Sexual intercourse or sexual acts by a man with his own wife, the wife not being under 15 years of age, is not rape." This means that the wife being above the age of 15 cannot claim it under a criminal offense.

The age of consent for the child bride was increased to 15 years in the case of Phulmoni Dasi (also known as Queen-Empress vs. Hari Mohan Maiti),1886. Where the child-wife was raped by her husband, despite the age of the child being 11 years and the age of the husband being around 35. Though the autopsy report claimed the child died out of vaginal rupture, the husband was acquitted from Rape charges, as accordingly the penal code excluded marital rape and allowed a man to have sexual intercourse with his wife, as long she had attained 10 years of age.

But in the specific case, the court held that the man cannot enjoy the child as his wife when he had no concern for her health and safety. This case triggered the government to amend the Age of consent to be raised to 12 years. Later the Amendment act, of 1925 was enacted to raise the age of consent for the bride to 13 and 14 years respectively. Later on,in the case-law of Infinite thoughts v. Union of India[iii], the court held that if the wife is aged between 15 to 18 years, the husband is still convicted for rape. But this sadly gives the spouse an exception to rape women above the age of 18. The woman being a wife accepts that her husband has all sorts of control over her. The victim has nowhere to approach, as the law doesn't recognize it as a criminal offense, nor does the family of the victim.

The Constitutional Validity of Spousal/Marital Rape

At present the Delhi H.C is hearing a challenge regarding the Constitutional validity of the immunity provided by Section 375 of the Indian Penal Code 1872 for Marital Rape.

The petitioners claim that Marital Rape stands against all the fundamental rights guaranteed under Article 21, Article 19, and Article 14. The immunity guaranteed by sec 375 stands against the Right to Personal Autonomy of a woman, the right to life with dignity, and the Right to equality. This law creates an unnecessary classification between married women and unmarried women. It simply eliminates the Right of married women to give consent to sexual activity. Even when a sex worker has a right to say no or in other words, non-consensual intercourse will amount to rape even in the case of sex workers but not for married women cause here culture is given greater importance than consent.

This creates an outrage among the feminine society as numerous women get exploited by their husbands. Marriage being a custom does not entitle the husband the control over the wife. Consent is essential despite the relationship the victim shares with the rapist. Marital rape is still not considered taboo in the first place to be emphasized as a criminal offense, as society thinks that the wife is married to her husband, devotes herself completely, and is obliged by the actions of her husband. But marriage is a cultural institution that develops the idea of a man and woman living together rather not owning the rights of the other person.

<u>INDIAN LEGISLATION ON MARITAL RAPE</u>

The United Nations Committee on Elimination of Discrimination Against Women in the year 2013 recommended India criminalize marital rape. But the then UPA lead government failed to change the law. But now after becoming the opposition, its chief Rahul Gandhi, has tweeted in favor of striking down the immunity given by sec 375 for Marital Rape.

Not only the United Nations, even the J.S Verma Committee which was set up after the Nirbhaya case[iv],alsorecommended the criminalization of Marital Rape. Yet the then UPA government failed to strike down the immunity.

Similar to the UPA government, the NDA government that's currently in power, has also opposed the criminalization of Marital Rape in its Affidavit filed before the High court of Delhi. So now it's clear that trusting the legislature won't solve this problem of Marital Rape. It's high time the judiciary intervenes and criminalizes marital rape.

According to the UN Population Fund, more than 66 percent of the married women in India aged between 15 to 49 have either been forced or in some cases even been beaten for providing sex, irrespective of their socio-economic position. According to the International Men and Gender Equality Survey, 2011at least 20 percent of the husbands would have forced their spouse for sexual intercourse.

<u>**CONCLUSION**</u>

From the above data, it's clear that marital rape is still prevalentin many families. This kind of heinous crime is still not criminalized in India. The victim has no institution to approach, asthe concept of Marital rape is still not criminalized in India. This type ofutterly odious crime cannot be treated as domestic violence, as the severity of the crime equals rape and cannot be provided an exception, just because the victim is already married to the rapist.

It is stated that the phrase Culture over Consent should be emphasized and followed. Peoplethink that the concept of Marital Rape is against the institution of marriage. Even, our former Chief Justice of India, Ms. Dipak Misra"because it will create absolute anarchy in families and our country is sustaining itself because of the family platform which upholds family values," wasquotedto Deccan Herald by Misra[v]. Statements like these overhold culture over humanity. But in many cases, the SC did not consider culture for justice. For instance, the SC in the case of Navtej Singh Johar v. Union of India[vi] made Sec.377 unconstitutional and allowed consensual sex between adults of the same sex. This was against the culture and yet the SC took a decision to respect human feelings and render justice for the Homosexuals.

Also, in the case of Jit Kumari Pangeni (Neupane) and Others v. Prime Ministers and Council of Ministers and Others[vii],The Nepal SC held that punishing marital rape differently from other rapes will amount to the breach of equal rights provision in the Interim constitution. Hence, even when it didn't have the power to change sentencing terms, it directed the authorities to change the term of sentencing for marital rape equaling to that of a rape. This case proves the severity of marital rape.

Cases like this open up a gateway for the government to criminalizeMarital rape. When it recognizes Marital rape as a criminal offense for the victim below the age of 18, it is also required to consider rape for victims above the age of 18, as an entitlement of a relationship will not reduce the severity of rape and will still amount to a criminal offense. The immunization of marital rape which was originated from the colonial laws itself emanated the immunity. Then, it's high time India takes the necessary steps to criminalize Marital rape.

CASE SUMMARY: SHREYA SINGHAL VS. UNION OF INDIA AIR 2015 SC 1523

Author: Jay Kumar Gupta, I year of B.B.A.,LL.B.(Hons.) from NMIMS School of Law, Bengaluru

<u>INTRODUCTION</u>

The judicial review[i] of section 66A of the IT Act 2000[ii] is the subject of this lawsuit. In plain terms, judicial review is the power granted to the Supreme Court and High Courts to examine the legality of any law enacted by the legislature. And if the law is found to be breaking the constitution's basic structure during the review, the court can strike down the law or any specific section of the law that is ambiguous, vague, or violates the constitution's basic structure by using the judicial review power[iii].Article 13 of the Indian Constitution[iv] specifically mentions the power of judicial review.[v]Article 141 of the Indian constitution[vi], which deals with the enforceability of supreme court judgements, reflects the concept of judicial review.[vii] It states that the Supreme Court of India's judgments are binding and enforceable in the courts that are subordinate to the it. This case might also question over separation of powers. The separation of powers principle asserts that the three branches of government (legislature, executive, and judiciary) will operate with checks and balances.[viii] Judicial review gives the judiciary an advantage over the legislature. In India, there is no idea of parliamentary review, in which the legislature can review judicial decisions. Reviewing, criticising, and overturning laws enacted by the legislature could be an infraction of the division of powers principle.

<u>FACTS</u>

The Information Technology Act of 2000[ix] (also known as the "IT Act") came into operation in the year 2000.The legislature voted in 2009 to include "Cyber Crimes" in the IT Act. As a result, a legislative amendment was approved to address the issue. The Information Technology Act's Section 66A, allows police to make arrests based on their own personal judgement of whether anything is "offensive" or "menacing."[x]

In this case, two women were arrested over a Facebook post in which they questioned the propriety of shutting down Mumbai City for the burial of a deceased politician. The arrest was made under Section 66A of the IT Act, citing the inflammatory and disagreeable nature of the posts.[xi]

Despite the fact that the police ultimately released them and dropped all charges against them, it became a topic of discussion, with many news outlets reporting the story and numerous conversations taking place. In the meantime, Shreya Singhal has filed a challenge in the Supreme Court, contesting the constitutional legality and functionality of Section 66A of the IT Act, claiming that it breaches Article 19(1)(a)[xii] of the Indian Constitution, which guarantees freedom of expression[xiii].

<u>ISSUES</u>

The question in this case was whether Section 66A of the IT Act is constitutionally valid or whether it breaches Article 19(1)(a) of the Indian Constitution, which guarantees freedom of expression.

These are the points on which petitioner had challenged the section 66A of the IT Act:

It violates the fundamental right of freedom of speech and expression. Moreover, none of the eight subjects are secured by the article 19(2)[xiv].This section in creating an offence suffers from the vice of vagueness because of which the innocent persons are roped in as offenders.[xv]The execution of the previously mentioned portion would be a unobtrusive kind of censorship, undermining an essential esteem revered in Article 19(1)(a)[xvi]. Inasmuch as there's no perceivable distinction between those who utilize the web and those who utilize their strategies of communication through words talked or composed, the said arrangement encroaches on the rights of people beneath Articles 14[xvii] and 21[xviii] of the Indian Constitutions[xix].

ARGUMENTS

ARGUMENTS GIVEN BY PETITIONER

Section 66A of the Information Technology Act violates article 19(1)a of the Indian Constitution, which states that freedom of expression is a fundamental right. This part is very vague and vulnerable because the section's boundary isn't established, and the numerous terminologies employed there, aren't defined clearly.[xx] It grants law enforcement agents complete discretion in interpreting these laws based on their own personal interpretations and assessments. This section does not define limitation. The petitioner also stated that these laws are arbitrary, subjective and nebulous. It can be used by various governments for their own self-interests by limiting people's ability to object to government policies and raise their voices, which is in violation of Article 21 of the Indian Constitution, which protects life and personal liberty. The petitioner further claimed that this provision lacks "intelligible differentia" or "difference capable of being understood," as required by Article 14 of the Indian Constitution. Different people will understand this regulation differently. As a result, this also breaches article 14[xxi].

ARGUMENTS GIVEN BY RESPONDENTS

Respondents objected the maintainability of the writ petition filed by the petitioner in this matter. The legal borders of the legislative and the judiciary were a point of contention among respondents.[xxii] They said that the legislature's job is to answer the people's wishes, and that the court can only intervene if part III of the Indian constitution is violated. Part III of the Indian Constitution contains articles 12 to 35 that deal with people' basic fundamental rights. They claimed that the entire writ petition was politically motivated and could not be sustained. They questioned the petitioner's reasoning, in which she protested to the section's vagueness. Respondent argued that while the statute was arbitrary in character, this should never be used to declare it unconditionally null and void. They said that the entire argument of the petitioner is based on the assumption that this part may violate citizens' fundamental rights. They went on to say that these presumptions should not be used as a basis for declaring a legislation unconstitutional[xxiii].

JUDGEMENTS

What may be objectionable to one person may not be objectionable to another, according to the court. The court went on to say that even if various legal/judicial minds have different opinions and conclusions on the same information, how can law enforcement agencies decide which should be considered objectionable and which should not? The petitioner's argument about the vagueness of terms like "annoying," "inconvenient," and "grossly insulting" used in section 66A was accepted by the court. The court acknowledged that defining the law's boundaries and elements is difficult.[xxiv] Finally, the Court concurred with the notion that it violates Indian constitution's article 19(a)1, which deals with freedom of expression and free speech. As a result, the Court declared section 66 A of the IT Act, 2000 "unconstitutional" and a breach of free speech and expression.[xxv]

POSITIVES OF THE JUDGEMENT

The legislature will be more careful about ambiguity when framing new laws.Ambiguity and vagueness in the law will be reduced.Law will be in accordance with the basic structure of the constitution.The respect and reverence of the judiciary have increased in the eyes of the common people.People willsee judiciary as the guardian of their fundamental rights.It establishes the rule of law.Nothing can be done in arbitrariness.Law is the supreme.It gives new light to the freedom of speech and expression.People can now fearlessly can object the policies of the government through any medium it seems fit to them without any fear of prosecution by the government.

NEGATIVES OF THE JUDGEMENT

Some argue that this decision goes against the notion of separation of powers, which states that the three wings of governance must act independently with checks and balances in order to function properly. It may be undemocratic to overturn a law passed by a majority vote in parliament.Parliamentarians are chosen through a fair electoral system.As a result, the laws enacted by the legislature represent the support and faith of the people from whom they are elected.As a result, striking down the entire legislation or a specific section of the law through judicial review may be contrary to the general will of the people for whom the law was enacted.

<u>CONCLUSION</u>

It's not as if the entire section 66A was repealed. Only those provisions are struck down that, according to the honourable court, violate article 19(1)(a) and are not protected under article 19(2). While the provision dealing with the barring of public access to information, as well as section 79, was found to be constitutional and legal. The nature of Section 66A was ambiguous, and the terms utilised there were similarly open to interpretations. Court found there was no link of it with causing any sort of disturbance or any kind of incitement of violence, hence they struck it down. The court stated that no one can take away citizens' fundamental rights under such circumstances, and that this clause did not comply with Article 19 of the Constitution (2). As a result, it is unconstitutional.

<u>Author's Biography</u>

Author is a first year student at NMIMS School of Law,Bengaluru. He is pursuing BBA LL.B.(Hons.). He is very hard working and dedicated to his work.He has good researching skills and writing abilities.

CHAPTER FIVE

TYPES OF ADR WITH REFERNCE TO LOK ADALAT UNDER INDIAN LAW

Author: Tanveer Sethi, IV year of B.B.A.,LL.B.(Hons.) (International trade & investment laws) from University of Petroleum and Energy Studies, School of Law, Dehradun.

Co-author: Sarthak Pant, III year of B.A.,LL.B.(Hons.) from Ideal Institute of Management and Technology and School of Law, Delhi (GGSIPU)

Tanveer Sethi

Sarthak Pant

ABSTRACT

The Indian legal executive is one of the most established legal frameworks. With the progression of time, the framework has become wasteful to manage forthcoming cases. Indian courts are obstructed with long agitated cases, thus dissecting such a circumstance calls for development to concoct a superior other option, as many cases are as yet forthcoming and this calls for grave consideration. Considering the Indian situation one might say that ADR assumes a critical part by its different strategies, in conquering the issue of pendency of cases . It tends to be additionally said that ADR-Alternate Dispute Mechanism gives an advantageous approach to settling disputes. There is no court cost payable when a matter is reported in a Lok Adalat. If a matter impending in the court of guideline is suggested the Lok Adalat and is settled appropriately, the court cost at first paid in the court on the fights/demand is moreover limited back to the social affairs. Individuals closing the cases in the Lok Adalats are known as the Members of the Lok Adalats, they fill the role of legal conciliators just and don't have any legitimate influence; as such they can persuade the social affairs to show up at a goal for settling the dispute outside the court in the Lok Adalat and won't pack or power any of the get-togethers to mull over settle cases or matters either clearly or by suggestion.

INTRODUCTION

Lok Adalat is one of the alternative dispute redressal mechanisms, it is a gathering where disputes/cases forthcoming in the court of regulation or at pre-suit stage are settled/compromised genially. Lok Adalats have been given statutory status under the Legal Services Authorities Act, 1987. Under the said Act, the honor (choice) made by the Lok Adalats is considered to be a pronouncement of a civil court and is conclusive and restricting on all parties and no allure against such an honor lies under the watchful eye of any court of regulation.

In the event that the gatherings are not happy with the honor of the Lok Adalat however there is no arrangement for an allure against such an honor, yet they are allowed to start case by moving toward the court of proper ward by recording a case by following the expected methodology, in exercise of their entitlement to dispute.

The Lok Adalat will not conclude the matter so alluded at its own example, rather similar would be settled based on the trade off or settlement between the gatherings. The individuals will help the gatherings in an autonomous and fair way in their endeavor to arrive at genial settlement of their dispute.

Lok Adalat is an arrangement of an allotment of equity which has appeared to wrestle with the issue of giving modest and expedient judges to individuals. Lok Adalat as the very name proposes implies individuals' court. Lok represents individuals and the Adalat implies court.

<u>NATURE AND SCOPE</u>

Generally speaking, Lok Adalat isn't a court in its acknowledged meaning. The distinction between Lok Adalat and regulation court is that the law court sets at its premises where the prosecutors accompany their attorneys and witnesses goes to individuals to conveys equity at their entryway step. It is a discussion given by individuals themselves or by invested individuals including social exercises or social dissident lawful aiders, and public energetic individuals having a place with different social statuses. It is only a firm discussion gave by individuals themselves to empowering the commoners to ventilate their complaints against the state organizations or against different residents and to look for a fair settlement if conceivable.

The essential way of thinking behind the Lok Adalat is to determine individuals dispute by conversation, directing, influence and placation so it gives rapid and modest equity, common and free assent of the gatherings. In short it is a party's equity where individuals and judges take part and resolve their disputes by conversation, influence and shared assent.

<u>Kinds of cases at Lok Adalat</u>

1. Mutation of land cases.
2. Compoundable criminal offences.
3. Family disputes.
4. Encroachment on forest lands.
5. Land acquisition disputes.
6. Motor accident claim, and
7. Cases which are not sub-judice.

Resources and achievement of Lok Adalat: Lok Adalat can only expect gratitude of the people in distress in return. They must devote time for the cause of social justice and dedicate their service for its success. Lok Adalats are generally organized in the premises of courts. Lok Adalat can work as real good substitutes for setting cases which are pending in superior courts. Encouraged by the response that Lok Adalat have been receiving at the district level, the state legal aid boards have started organizing Lok Adalats for cases pending in the High Courts.

The Lok Adalat has also been organized even for the cases pending in the Supreme Court. Lok Adalats are known as Peoples festivals of justice because settlements are not always necessarily according to legal principles settlements have an eye mainly on - Social goals like ending quarrels, Restoring family peace and Providing succor for destitute.

<u>ORGANIZATION OF LOK ADALAT</u>

The State Authority and District Authority, as well as the Supreme Court Legal Services Committee, the High Court Legal Services Committee, and the Taluk Legal Services Committee (Section 19 of Legal Services Authorities Act, 1987), can hold Lok Adalats whenever and however long they see fit. Each Lok Adalat arranged thusly should incorporate the accompanying:

1. Judicial officials, both dynamic and resigned
2. Other people, as might be determined.

Different people alluded in condition (b) of sub-segment (2) for Lok Adalats coordinated by the Supreme Court Legal Services Committee will have such insight and capabilities as the Central Government might endorse in conference with the Chief Justice of India for Lok Adalats coordinated by the Supreme Court Legal Services Committee. The State Government, in interview with the Chief Justice of the High Court, may recommend the experience and capabilities of others alluded to in condition (b) of sub-area (2) for Lok Adalats other than those alluded to in sub-segment (3).

A Lok Adalat has the power to decide and arrive at a trade off or settlement between the gatherings to a dispute in the accompanying regions:

- any beforehand forthcoming claim
- any case that falls under the ward of a court for which the Lok Adalat is coordinated however isn't introduced before it:

In any case, the Lok Adalat has no ward over any case or subject including an offense that isn't deserving of regulation.

COGNIZANCES OF CASES BY LOK ADALAT (SECTION 20)

The lok adalat can take discernment of issues in two distinct ways.

- At the point when the two players make an application for the make a difference to be moved to a lok adalat, or when one of the gatherings makes such an application, the court can move the case to lok adalats based on by all appearances fulfillment that the case is good for move.

- In the subsequent occurrence, in the event that the court figures it vital, it can allude the case to the Lok Adalat on suo witticism. The court will possibly move a case assuming the gatherings have been offered a sensible chance to be heard.

There are three modes that will be utilized to decide the case.

- It still up in the air in the initial mode by considering equity, decency, value, and the law.
- It still up in the air in the subsequent mode by compelling the gatherings to agree or think twice about.

The case will be alluded back to the courtroom in the event that no trade off is advertised. The procedures will start right when the reference was made.

PROCEDURE OF LOK ADALAT

The method utilized at a Lok Adalat is genuinely direct and it dislike the system utilized in courts.

- The two players to the dispute could document the Application, or the gatherings to the dispute could verbally specify the make a difference to the Court during the conference to allude the make a difference to Lok Adalat.
- Any party might document an application to allude the make a difference to Lok Adalat, and the Court, in the wake of hearing all parties, may allude the case to Lok Adalat assuming at first sight fulfilled that there are potential open doors for settlement.
- Lok Adalat would act rapidly to arrive at a trade off or settlement between the gatherings, directed by the standards of equity, value, reasonableness, and other lawful contemplations.
- The case will be gotten back to the Court that alluded it assuming no trade off or settlement can be reached. The case will then, at that point, be heard in court, beginning from where the reference was made.

In addition, the gatherings are not constrained to pay any court charges. The gatherings can be addressed by their own legitimate direction, however on the off chance that they can't bear the cost of one under any circumstance, the Legal Aid Committee can give one.

<u>Award of Lok-Adalat (Sec. 21)</u>

1. Every honor of the Lok Adalat will be considered to be a declaration of civil court or by and large, a request for some other court and where a trade off or a settlement has been shown up at, by a Lok Adalat for a situation alluded to it under sec. 20(1), the court charge paid in such case will be discounted in a way given under the court expense Act, 1870.

2. Even honor made by a Lok Adalat will be conclusive and restricting on every one of the gatherings to the dispute and no allure will deceive any court against the honor.

<u>Powers of Lok Adalat (Sec. 22)</u>

1. The Lok-Adalat will have similar abilities as are vested in a civil court under the code of civil technique 1908 while attempting a suit in regard of the accompanying issues specifically;

- The calling and authorizing the participation of any observer and inspecting him on pledge.
- The revelation and creation of any report.
- The gathering of proof on testimonies.

- The ordering of any openly available report or archive or duplicate of such record or archive from any court of office.
- Such different issues as might be endorsed.

2. Without bias to the consensus of the powers contained in sub sec. (1), each Lok Adalat will have the imperative abilities to indicate its own system for the assurance of any dispute preceding it.

3. All procedures before the Lok Adalat will be considered to be legal actions inside the importance of sec. 193, 219 and 228 of the I.P.C and each Lok-Adalat will considered to be civil with the end goal of sec. 195 of C. P C.

Functions of the Lok Adalat

Lok Adalat can acknowledge just such cases as gone in close vicinity to their skill and ability for removal. The development towards getting sorted out of Lok-Adalats appeared in regard of a couple of chosen matters. All their underlying working they engaged engine vehicle mishap causes and requests associated with them. It is ideally expected that the Lok Adalats would acknowledge different causes additionally among them being residency matters, cash causes, so that such disputes are chosen individual bonds or under takings.

This will be sign of the way that in the questions of goal of disputes, India has returned to its conventional strategies. In any case, all things considered experience has shown that it isn't not difficult to carry the gatherings to dispute to the exchange table and to request that they settle under some sort of give and take including compromise.

Countless lawful causes are to such an extent that one of the gatherings is keen on delaying prosecution and just different needs a rapid preliminary. Apparently by this approach the state would be saved of unnecessary expenses of suit and furthermore good for nothing authoritative accumulations. Government needs to bear many immediate and aberrant expense of prosecution. In the class of direct of expenses, the expenses are court and legal advisors charges, costs of indictment and of taking care of accidental matters.

Circuitous expenses are loss of time engaged with disputes and expanding expenses of consuming guardian. There are a few classifications of government suit in which Lok Adalats can assume a productive part. One of such classifications is matter emerging out of land obtaining. Among individuals whose land is obtained are for the most part unfortunate townspeople those having a place with working classes. Whenever their property is removed, from their hands, they normally with the exception of that remuneration ought to be given to them at the earliest development of time.

One more class of government case which can be taken care of through Lok Adalats is disciplinary procedure. Numerous procedures in this class are such in which the reason for dispute is exceptionally basic, the foundation is additionally extremely clear and there isn't discussion about it yet the gatherings can't come out transparently however the time factor continues aggregating complexity. For instance with holding of annuity and other retirement benefits. Work disputes are one more class in which Lok Adalats can assume sound part. The apparatus of pacification and neighborly settlements accessible under the Industrial dispute Legislations which has been by and large fruitful in settling unnecessary contentions Lok Adalats would be a superior structure even in some help disciplinary issues.

Other forms of Lok-Adalats

1. Mini Lok Adalat: Legal aid camps or Lok-Adalats at sub-district level and in villages are like forums, functioning in rural areas especially to cater to rural and tribal people competently and at their door steps to resolve disputes with all the expediency.

2. Village Courts: These are units of self government they are like village Panchayats administration is a state subject hence state Panchayats Raj institutions enactments come into play, giving rise to village courts under articles 40 of our Constitution.

3. Mediation Centre's: These mediating Centres's were started in the year 1983 in Tamil Nadu legal aid and advice Board.

4. Centre's for women: To give a special status to women and their exclusive problems Tamil Nadu state gave thrust and expansion to women mediation Centre's by starting such Centre's exclusively for women their role is to deal with matrimonial problems. They also help in setting disputes involving women. They promote nights of women family matters get special attention of; a) Voluntary agencies b) Professionals.

5. Mobile Lok Adalats are also organized in various parts of the country which travel from one location to another to resolve disputes in order to facilitate the resolution of disputes through this mechanism.

Conclusion

Lok Adalat is extremely successful in repayment of cash claims. Disputes like parcel suits, harms and marital cases can likewise be effortlessly settled before Lok Adalat, as the extension for compromise through a methodology of compromise is high in these cases. A Lok Adalat can take up civil cases (counting marriage, and family disputes) and compoundable crook cases

First time lok adalat was held in Gujrat in 1999. It is a gathering where cases forthcoming on panchayat or at pre case stage in a court of regulation are settled. They have been given statutory status under the Legal Services Authorities Act, 1987.

Under this Act, the honor (choice) made by the Lok Adalats is considered to be an instance of a civil court and is conclusive and restricting on all parties and no allure against such an honor lies under the watchful eye of any court of regulation. In the event that the gatherings are not happy with the honor of the Lok Adalat (however there is no arrangement for an allure against such an honor), they are allowed to start suit by moving toward the court of fitting purview.

CHAPTER SIX

SEAT-VENUE CONCERNS WHEN THE ARBITRATION AGREEMENT IS SILENT: JUDICIAL ANALYSIS

Author: Adv. Harshit Adwani, LL.M. from Maharashtra National Law University, Nagpur

Co-author: Vishakha Gupta, LL.M. from Maharashtra National Law University, Nagpur

ABSTRACT

Overburdened judiciary and delay in the decisions have increased the dependency on alternate dispute resolution (ADR) mechanism for resolving the disputes, especially in the corporate world. However, it is to be noted that these methods have certain issues, which come to light after implementation. One of such issues is confusion regarding seat and venue of arbitration. This confusion intensifies when the agreement is silent on these clauses. The present article deals with two recent judgments of Supreme Court and High Court, and analyses how judiciary has dealt with this issue, to ensure that the popularity of arbitration proceedings among people remains unaffected.

INTRODUCTION – SEAT AND VENUE

The concept of 'seat' and 'venue' in arbitration is considered to be one of the biggest impediments in the progress of arbitration proceedings. Due to lack of legal knowledge, parties tend to forget to designate a place as 'seat' of arbitration in the agreement,[i] which leads to a sense of confusion[ii] in respect of the place of arbitration and the applicable law. The terms 'seat' and'venue' have not been defined under the Arbitration and Conciliation Act, 1996 [hereinafter 'the Arbitration Act']. Instead,it deals with 'Place of arbitration' underSection 20 of the Act.[iii]In real-world applicationscenarios, 'seat' is the place where the arbitration proceedings are anchored,[iv] It helps in determining the laws applicable for governing arbitral proceedings (lex arbritri),[v]whereas the term 'venue' is related to the geographicallocation decided by the parties for conductingthe arbitration proceedings. While dealing with this issue, judiciary has made significant efforts to create a line of differentiation between the two concepts.[vi]However, the issue intensifies when the agreement is silent on the 'seat' or 'venue' of the arbitration, as it effects the jurisdictional aspect for regulation of arbitral proceedings.

<u>BGS SGS SOMA JV v. NHPC LTD.[vii]: WHEN AGREEMENT IS SILENT ON 'SEAT' OF ARBITRATION</u>

The parties entered into a contract of construction. The agreement contained a clause for dispute resolution, which specified that the Arbitration Proceedings shall be held at New Delhi/Faridabad, India. As dispute arose between the parties, the Petitioner issued a notice of arbitration to the Respondent, and dispute was referred to arbitral tribunal, constituted in New Delhi, which delivered an award in favour of the Petitioner. The award was challenged before the Court of District and Sessions Judge, Faridabad,against which the Petitioner filed an application, contending that the appropriate court to entertain such application wouldbe either the court of New Delhi (which was the seat of arbitration) or District Judge at Dhemaji, Assam (where the cause of action arose). The court returned sec. 34 application to be filed before the appropriate court i.e. the court at New Delhi. The Respondent filed an appeal before the High Court of Punjab and Haryana, which and held that court of Faridabad shall have jurisdiction, as Delhi is only a convenient venue where arbitral proceedings were held and not the seat of the arbitration proceedings. Aggrieved by the judgement, the petitioner filed a special leave petition before the Supreme Court of India.

The Supreme Court in this case observed that choice of seat is akin to an exclusive jurisdiction clause.[viii] It was further noted that if the concept of concurrent jurisdiction is accepted, it will empower the party to approach any court, other than the court at the agreed upon seat, which might cause great inconvenience, and might defeat the general expectations of other party. As a result, the Court held that when any place is specified as a 'venue' in an arbitration agreement, it can be considered as a 'seat' of arbitration, as venue is related to the arbitration proceedings as a whole.

AARKA SPORTS MANAGEMENT PVT. LTD. v. KALSI BUILDCON PVT. LTD.[ix]:WHERE AGREEMENT IS SILENT ON 'SEAT' AS WELL AS 'VENUE'

The petitioner, in this case, Aarka Sports Management filed a petition in the Delhi High Court, requesting for appointment of an arbitrator under Section11 of the Arbitration Act. Though the respondent (Kalsi Buildcon) did not dispute the existence of agreement or notice of invocation, they challenged the jurisdiction of the Delhi High Court to entertain the said petition.

The petitioner relied on the main agreement signed by the parties along with judicial precedents,[x]and argued that the parties mutually provided the exclusive jurisdiction to the courts in Delhi under clause 15 of the agreement and so the High Court of Delhi is empowered to entertain and decide on the petition.To this, the respondent highlighted that the agreement was drawn in Ranchi, signed in Lucknow and executed in Patna. In this way, neither the cause of action arose in Delhi, nor did the agreement contain any provision specifying Delhi to be the seat of arbitration. On the other hand. The respondent relied on the case of Interglobe Aviation Limited v. N. Satchidanand,[xi] and argued that parties are not empowered to confer jurisdiction on a Court, which otherwise has no jurisdiction.

The Court analysed relevant provisions of the Act related to the court of competent jurisdiction,[xii] and place of arbitration,[xiii]along with various judgments referred by both the parties and held that Section20 of the Act confers power in the hands of parties to choose a 'neutral seat of arbitration'. In other words, the choice of seat of arbitration is not restricted by provisions of the Code of Civil Procedure,[xiv]and parties can choose a place as a seat, even where no cause of action arose at that place. Moreover,Courtclarified that when a place is selected as a seat of arbitration, the court of that place would have exclusive jurisdiction to regulate the arbitration proceedings.

However, the position is differentwhen no place is chosen as the seat of arbitration by the parties. In this situation, Section 20(2) of the Act will come into play, under which the arbitral tribunal will have the authority to determine the seat of arbitration.Regarding the court competent to have jurisdiction in such cases, the court held that "If the parties have not agreed on the seat of the arbitration, the Court competent to entertain an application under Section 11 of the Arbitration and Conciliation Act would be the "Court" as defined in Section 2(1) (e) of the Act read with Sections 16 to 20 of the Code of Civil Procedure."[xv]

Considering this principle, the Court held that not designating Delhi as the seat of arbitrationto entertain sec. 11 petition. The courtobserved that the petitioner could have succeeded if the agreement had provided the seat of arbitration to be Delhi, as it would have provided exclusive jurisdiction to the courts of Delhi to entertain and decide the application. The court also noted that parties are not empowered to confer jurisdiction on the Court, which otherwise had no jurisdiction.

CONCLUSION

In several instances, Judges from the Supreme Court and High Courts have shared their perception on the active role played by ADR in the protection of rights and access to justice. According to Justice S.B. Sinha, ADR is an age-old principle, roots of which can be identified in ancient India.[xvi] Recent statements by former[xvii] and current Chief Justice of India[xviii] can be referred to recognize the significance of ADR methods in dispute resolution in a contemporary situation.

Though the Court has specified in BGS SGS Soma case that the law laid down under Hardy Exploration case is not a good law, the former judgment canhave a negative impact on the existingarbitration system in the country.[xix] Experts have opined that ruling laid down in BGS SGS Somacase can create a lot of confusion, as it ignores the principles laid down in previous precedents. Also, considering 'venue' as 'seat' of arbitration would affect the 'judicial seat' in case of any change in 'venue' of arbitration, which is contrary to the view taken in BALCO case.[xx] Though it is argued that BGS SOMA case can create a clear path for future cases, the judgment laid down in Mankatsu Impex Private Limited v. Airviual Limited,[xxi] further adds to the existing blurriness.

Contrary to this ongoing tussle, the Aarka Sports case is an ideal illustration of an attempt by the judiciary to fill the voids, which might arise while interpretation of seat and venue in an arbitration agreement. The judgment resolves the issue where no seat or venue is specified, which ultimately protects the interest of parties and helps in creating a flawless system, which will guide the parties to approach the competent authority in future events. As Supreme Court has not deliberated or analysed any case with similar facts, the judgment holds a precedential value.

CHAPTER SEVEN

AR AND VR APPLICATIONS IN MEDICAL SCIENCES

Author: K. Anil Kumar Reddy, III year of Btech(Electronics and communication engineering) from Christ University,Bangalore

Currently, the medical applications of Augmented Reality (AR) and virtual reality (VR) are found mainly within the following six areas: educational training, clinical assistance, impairment, psychological disorders, rehabilitation training, and personalized fitness. as an example, AR/VR is sometimes used for medical education or surgical simulation training; AR is sometimes accustomed assist surgery or guiding robots to perform surgery; and VR is visiting be used for amblyopia treatment, rehabilitation training, and management of certain mental illnesses. Owing to the high capital input, the VR/AR market is anticipated to point to fast growth within the economic chain within the subsequent three to four years. Despite multiple application spaces of the VR/AR equipment within the longer term, we wish to create sure their compliance with certain safety codes in actual use, to appreciate the management of physical health. Compared to VR, which is utilized primarily for training and simulation, AR is more extensively utilized in medical operations. in line with the good data query of CB Insights, CrunchBase, and AngelList, there are now about 30 start-ups specializing in AR medical applications worldwide. Nine of them are financed, with a crammed with $552 million, revealing a 30% investment attraction rate. the appliance of AR in treatment remains within the exploration stage. Markets and Markets research group estimates that the medical VR market is predicted to grow to $5 billion by 2023 at a compound annual rate of growth of 36.6%.

VR and AR technologies applications

VR and AR technologies are now most actively utilized in medicine to rearrange and perform surgeries. Three-dimensional data from CT and MRI scans help to form a game model of a patient and steel onself for surgery taking into consideration risks and potential problems. Surgeons are using these machines for several years to rearrange for particularly complex interventions. For example, the VR-based Surgical Theater platform helps plan neurosurgical surgeries within the U.S. and Israel. Using this solution in 2021, Soroka center (Israel) performed the foremost complex surgery to separate twins with conjoined heads. Using Surgical Theater, doctors created interactive 3D and VR models that allowed them to review problem areas through a special headset. Next, the operation was designed. At the last stage, using SNAP (Surgical Navigation Advanced Platform), the created scheme was transferred to the surgical navigation system of the realm.

VR and AR solutions for Medicine in Testing and Research

For anesthesia, or rather to chop back pain; For treatment of dementia, system lesions, and mental disorders; To help the blind and visually impaired; To diagnose diseases, including Parkinson's disease; To develop communication skills moreover as empathy; VR and AR offer numerous benefits that help doctors. They also provide quality-of-life improvements for patients, including those with severe disorders, dementia, or other psychological conditions.

CHAPTER EIGHT

AGREEMENTS IN RESTRAINT OF MARRIAGE UNDER THE INDIAN CONTRACT ACT, 1872

Author: Khushi Bansal, I year of B.A.,LL.B. from Symbiosis Law School, NOIDA

<u>ABSTRACT</u>

Marriage is considered as a sacrosanct event. It is a social and legal union between a man and a women and their families. It is said that a new phase of a person's life starts when one gets married. It is important that no other person restricts someone from getting married in their life or not restrict the person from marrying a person of a particular caste or group. If something does such an act, it will be hit by Section 26 of the Indian Contract Act, 1872 which says that,"Every agreement in restraint of marriage of a person, other than a minor is void". This paper is organized in five parts. The first part gives a brief introduction about Section 26 of the contract act and the need for this provision. The second part explains the provisions of the agreements in restraint of marriage and a general exception to this section. The third part tries to make the topic clearer with the help of two Indian case laws. The fourth part examines how marriage brokerage agreement and contract of betrothal is different from agreements in restraint of marriage. The fifth and the last part explains the difference of the agreements in restraint of marriage between the English Contract Law and the Indian Contract Act.

INTRODUCTION

Section 26 of Indian Contract Act, 1872 deals with agreement in restraint of marriage. The verbatim says that, "Every agreement in restraint of the marriage of any person, other than a minor is void."[i]The Indian Contract Act became the first law in our country which had such provision. Rome was the first country in the world to declare these agreements as illegal.Agreement means the promises made between two parties having offer, acceptance and a consideration. Any agreement which stops or prevents a person from marrying is void in the eyes of law.

Let's take an illustration for better understanding:

A tells S, "I will give you 10 lakh rupees if you do not marry your entire life." S accepts this offer but after two years gets married. A after knowing about S's marriage files a suit against S. Do you think A will succeed? In this situation, A will not succeed as any agreement which stops a person from getting married is null and void as per law.

WHY WAS THIS PROVISION INTRODUCED?

This provision was introduced so that an adult person can marry a person of his/her choice which is also provided to a person under Article 21 of the Indian Constitution which is also a part of fundamental rights (Part III). Article 21 states that every person whether citizen or non-citizen has the right to personal liberty which also includes marrying a person of choice. Also, according to me it is ethically wrong to stop a person from marrying a person of his/her choice. It is a provision of law to discourage agreements which restraint freedom of marriage.[ii]

PROVISIONS OF AGREEMENTS IN RESTRAINT OF MARRIAGE UNDER INDIAN CONTRACT ACT, 1872

As we know that all the agreements which hinders a marriage are void, these agreements are of two types:

1. General Restraint- It means completely debarring a person from getting married.

Illustration: A father saying to her daughter not to marry her entire life. This kind of a restraint is a general restraint.

2. Partial Restraint- this means stopping a person for a specific period of time or for not marrying a particular person or a person of a particular caste.

Illustration: A father asking her daughter not to marry a person belonging to a person of other caste is a partial restraint.

GENERAL EXCEPTION TO SECTION 26

All agreements in restraint of marriage of minors is not considered as void as this is done for the minor's benefit by their parents or legal guardians. This means that any agreement which debars marriage of a person below 18 years of age is valid as per law.

Illustration 1: If X, a legal guardian of A stops her from marrying till she attains 18 years of age and A agrees to this. This agreement cannot be challenged in the courts. But, a parent or legal guardian can only restraint the person till 18 years of age. Once, the person attains 18 years of age, any such agreement will not be considered.

CASE LAWS RELATING TO AGREEMENTS IN RESTRAINT OF MARRIAGE

SHRAWAN KUMAR@PAPPU vs NIRMALA

High court of Judicature at Allahabad

4th December, 2012

Bench- Pankaj Mittal

Petitioner- Shrawan Kumar@Pappu

Respondent- Nirmala

FACTS- The petition reveals that the petitioner i.e., Shrawan alleges that his marriage was agreed to be solemnised with the respondent. But the respondent now wants to marry someone else and therefore the petitioner wanted permanent injunction to be passed restraining Nirmala from marrying anyone else except the petitioner.

JUDGEMENT PRONOUNCED BY THE COURT- The petition filed by Shrawan Kumar was dismissed by Pankaj Mittal saying that stopping

Nirmala from marrying the man of her own choice will be considered as restraint of marriage. He also said that a sacred institution like marriage cannot be forced upon or put a restraint. He said that 'Right to marry is a crucial part of right to life and liberty and is one of the fundamental rights.[iii]

RAO RANI vs GULAB RANI

Decided on 15th April 1942

High Court of Judicature at Allahabad

Bench- Justice Ahmed, then chief justice

Petitioner- Gulab Rani

Respondent- Rao Rani

FACTS- Both Rao Rani and Gulab Rani were widows, both of them had same husband named Ram Adhar. After their husband died, conflict arose between the two related to inheritance of zamindari land holdings. However, this dispute was finally settled by signing a compromise deed but the Revenue Court also stated that if any of the two would re-marry, then the entire land would go to the other one. Gulab Rani, however married again and so as per the judgement, entire land holding was transferred to Rao Rani. Years later, Gulab filed a suitin Allahabad High Court to regain her part of property claiming that the compromise deed was void as it prohibited her from marriage.

DECISION PRONOUNCED BY THE COURT- The then chief justice, Ahmed said that according to the court's order if any one of them would remarry, the entire property would be given to the other. Justice Ahmad said that no direct prohibition was imposed on either of them to re-marry and hence, it was not violative of Article 26 i.e., Agreement in restraint of marriage. Hence, the entire land holding was transferred to Rao Rani as she had not re-married unlike Gulab Rani.[iv]

<u>DIFFERENCE BETWEEN MARRIAGE BROKERAGE AGREEMENT, CONTRACT OF BETROTHAL AND RESTRAINT OF MARRIAGE</u>

Marriage brokerage agreement is the one in which a third party enters into an agreement with a party interested in marriage. The party interested in marrying tells about the specification of required partner and the broker finds as per the specification and gets paid for their work. The marriage companies like Jeevansathi are the marriage broker companies which enter into agreement with their customers and find the life partner for them and take money in turn. This will not be included in agreements in restraint of marriage as the third party is finding a suitable partner for their clients.

Contract of Betrothal means a promise in which parents or legal guardian consents to giving their girl in marriage to the groom of their choice. The girl's choice could also be same as the girl's choice. This is also not included as violative of Article 26 as there is no restriction not to marry anyone.

COMPARATIVE STUDY OF PROVISION OF AGREEMENTS IN RESTRAINT OF MARRIAGE UNDER ENGLISH CONTRACT LAW AND INDIAN CONTRACT ACT

Under the English Contract Law, the general restraint to marriage, other than that of a minor is completely prohibited which means completely preventing a person from getting married is prohibited. But, under English Contract Law agreements which are partial prohibition of marriage of a person, other than that of a minor is not completely void and is as per the discretion of courts.

But, as per Section 26 of Indian law of contract, all general and partial agreements in restraint of marriage, except a minor are void. The difference between the two are that Indian Act prohibits even partial restraint of marriage of adults but, under English law, agreements in partial restraint are not completely void.[v]

CONCLUSION

It can be concluded that according to Section 26 of Indian Contract Act, all the agreements in partial and general restraint of marriage are void. There is only one general exception and that is in the case of minors (people under 18 years of age). This provision was introduced so that people are given freedom to marry as per their choice. In both the case laws stated above, the judgement was in favour of respondents as in first case, court did not want to restraint Nirmala from marrying a person of choice and in second case, if re-marriage took place, the other spouse is debarred from assets of the dead spouse.

Also, both marriage brokerage agreement as well as betrothal contract are not considered as agreements in restraint of marriage. Lastly, there is difference in partial agreements related to restraint of marriage between contract laws in India and England.

'No one can stop us from marrying until we do so'

CHAPTER NINE

RULE OF ELECTION

Author: Aman Tiwari, IV year of B.A.,LL.B. from Delhi Metropolitan Education, Noida Affiliated to Guru Gobind Singh Indraprastha University, Delhi

<u>INTRODUCTION</u>

Voting refers to the ability to select from presumed alternatives. The idea of election protects both moveable and immovable property. In simple words, it means that if any person wishes to transfer any property over which he himself has no legal title then he must first notify the owner of the property, in order to give it away. It depends on the will of the property owner to allow it or deny it. Therefore, it should be considered that he has the authority to validate or reject a transaction using the theory of election.

For example:- Akash gives Mr. Seth his house as a present, and in the same transaction, Akash asks Mr. Seth to give his own shop to Simran. Seth has the choice of accepting or refusing the transfer. If Seth agrees to this transfer, he will be able to get the home but has to also give shop to Simran.

The Rule of Election is discussed in "Section 35 of the Transfer of Property Act". It is stipulated that when a property is transferred to an individual, the transferee has the option of accepting or rejecting the transferee. Along with the advantages of the transfer, the burden of the transfer is complementary.To put it another way, the legal principle "qui approbat non reprobate" states that a man cannot both approve and disapprove.

If the person who is scheduled to get a benefit denies it, the property that was due to be transferred to him reverts to the transferor, who is obligated to compensate the unhappy transferee. "If the transferor dies before the transferee can make an election, the transferor's legitimate heirs shall compensate the disappointed transferee from the inherited properties."[i]

"The Doctrine/Rule of election applies to all. In terms of the mode of elections, the owner's preference can be primary, by correspondence, or indirect. The acceptance of the benefit by the original owner is subject to conditions:

1. A person should have an electoral obligation of which he must be aware,
2. There must be proof of knowledge of the circumstances that could influence a reasonable man's decision.
3. Acceptance for a two-year term (Indian Succession Act, Section 188(1))
4. Status quo cannot be restored."[ii]

INGREDIENTS

- The transferor should not be the owner of the property.
- The transferor is liable to grant any of his property to the owner of the property, during the same time and also in the same instrument.
- The owner of the land may have a proprietary interest in it. Creditors are uncommitted to the referendum and only is capable of having a personal right which has to be paid by the debtor.
- Any individual who does not gains any profit directly in the transaction but gains it indirectly cannot be put up for election.

- The question regarding election does not arrive in the case where an owner is getting benefit in a separate role. For example, a person may recognise a bequest for a land while still having personal competence over the property.

<u>**RELEVANT CASE LAWS**</u>
COOPER V. COOPER
"The House of Lords clarified the theory of the doctrine of election in the landmark case of Cooper vs. Cooper."[iii]
FACTS OF THE CASE

- Two persons named Vera and Harold got married to each other in the year 1993. After their marriage, they had two children.After obtaining a mutual decree of separation, they also did a property settlement agreement where Vera was entitled to family house and automobile whereas Harold was entitled to tools along with the equipment's of the shop.
- The significant point here is that Vena was benefited from 4 initiatives in the name of Harold. As a consequence, the judge issued the divorce decree. After the decree was passed, Vena married Alves, and on the other side Harold married Ida. Because of remarriage, the benefit which was taken by Vera went to Ida as one policy was signed by Vera and not Harold. Harold later died.

ISSUE
"Whether vera and his children have a vested interest over the property?"
JUDGEMENT
"Since Harold's duty to support Vera under the terms of the divorce decree ended upon her remarriage, Vera had no interest in the policies at the time of Harold's death; and since the children's interest in their father's estate is limited to the amount necessary for their support as measured by the provisions of the divorce decree prior to reaching their majority, the children's interest in the estate of their father is limited to the amount necessary for their benefit as measured by the provisions of the divorce decree prior to reaching their majority."[iv]
"MUHAMMAD KADER ALI FAKIR V. FAKIR LAKMAN HAKIM"[v]

In another case the court explained the Doctrine of Election. The court explained that,

"The foundation of the doctrine of election is that a person taking the benefit of an instrument must also bear the burden, imposed thereby and that he cannot take under and against the same instrument. It is a breach to the general rule that no one may approbate or reprobate. The doctrine is based on intended intention to this extent that the law presumes that the author of an instrument intended to give effect to every part of it. There is an obligation on him who takes a benefit under a will or other instrument intended to give full effect to that instrument under which it was beyond the power of the donor or settler to dispose of, but to which effect can be given by the concurrence of him who receives the benefit under the same instrument, the law will impose on him who takes the benefit, the obligation of carrying the instrument into full and complete force and effect. If an instrument is invalid in part what remains is sufficient to put a person to his election if he claims a benefit under it."[vi]

EXCEPTION TO THE DOCTRINE OF ELECTION

As stated in Section 35 of the TP Act, if any person wishes to transfer his property to any other person he has to make a beneficiary provision for the concerned transferee after acknowledging the transfer. The transferee may then refuse the transferor's offer to take advantage of the beneficiary provision.However, there is an exception to this provision such that if the transferee does not give his or her clear permission or a definitive judgement, then the following situations will be added as he or she approves the transfer:

- Whether the transferee fully enjoys the beneficiary provision stated in the transfer, or fully enjoys the benefit, this would be known as transferee acceptance.
- If the transferee has not given his or her consent to the transfer of property after one year, the transferee is required to answer. If he or she does not do so, it would be presumed that he or she has given his or her approval to the move.
- In cases of disabilities, such as minority or lunacy, the duty of election may be revoked. Until their guardian makes the transfer.
- If the transferor creates a beneficiary clause as well as an independent beneficiary clause at the time of the convey. As a result, if the transferee does not consent to the transaction, the independent beneficiary clause

will be applied to him or her.

MODES OF ELECTION

1. Direct / Express
2. Indirect / Implied

The selected option is conveyed directly to the transferor in case of a direct election. However, in the case of indirect election, the selection is revealed by the transferee's conduct. There are three provisions for presumption under implied election: the advantage has been transferred and the person has enjoyed it for two years without taking any effort to waive the right; the person has no experience of election and has acknowledged the benefit; and the person has not taken any choice/ decision within one year of the transition.

CONCLUSION

"The Doctrine of Election" is outlined in "Section 35 of the Transfer of Property Act" of 1882. Using historic cases, this effort aims to answer the doctrine's multiple difficulties. This study has placed a special emphasis on presenting a clear picture of the conditions for the original owner's election to take place. If any individual wants to remove some property of any other person then the concept of common-law equity comes in play that forces a beneficiary to choose between keeping the property and adopting the device. "As a result, Section 35 states that an individual who does not gain directly from a transaction but benefits indirectly from it is not required to vote. Furthermore, a person who benefits from the transaction in one capacity may object to it in another."

Author's Bio

Penultimate Law Student passionate about enhancing knowledge at every step of life and a keen learner with an aim to expertise at everything.

CHAPTER TEN

AN ANALYSIS: FOREIGN TRADE (DEVELOPMENT AND REGULATION) ACT, 1992

Author: Ananaya Chauhan, IV year of B.A.,LL.B. from Delhi Metropolitan Education, Noida Affiliated to Guru Gobind Singh Indraprastha University, Delhi

Imports along with the exports are two major components of international trade. Foreign commerce is defined as the transfer of

commodities and amenities between two or more nations across international boundaries. The former refers to the physical flow of products into one country from another in a lawful way whereas the latter talks about the legal and physical transfer of commodities and services out of the nation. As a result, due to both imports and exports, world is turned in a local market.

"Foreign trade, often known as international trade", is critical for the survival of a brand as well as the prosperity of any country. This is because overseas commerce is one of the most important economic drivers for that particular company. Not only that, but international commerce is also expected to meet a country's demand for certain resources while also getting rid of excess resources that are readily accessible in the nation.

"With the help of Foreign trade, country has always developed in a way where it can address itself on an international platform, whether it is the most efficient use of resources, division of labour, specialization in a product, equality between prices, the quality of goods along with the multiple choices given or the country's overall economic growth."[i]The exporting, importing, and exporting involved in any country's overseas commerce serves to increase the people's quality of life. These types of international commerce also serve to preserve the country's payment solution balance and ensure that the economy is continually flowing freely.

Globalization has reached its pinnacle, and as a result, a lot of nations have implemented their own international trade rules in order to minimize any complications that may arise while trading with other nations. As a result, India, just like other countries around the world, has developed its own foreign policy that incorporates all of the know-hows and aspects of dealing with other nations.

<u>INTRODUCTION</u>

"The Foreign Trade (Development and Regulation) Act, 1992" governs and regulates India's foreign policy. On the "7th of August in the year 1992", this Act was enacted. The Act was not enacted as a new piece of legislation to govern foreign policy, but rather as a substitute for the Import and Exports (Control) Act of 1947. The Foreign Trade (Development and Regulation) Act, 1992 now regulates and manages India's whole export and import scenario. This act has removed all of the intricacies of the previous legislation and has given the Indian government some of the most powerful control tools available. This act is regarded as the most important piece of law governing the country's international commerce. The Act was enacted with the primary goal of providing an appropriate framework for the growth and standardization of international commerce by facilitating imports and increasing exports in the country, as well as any other concerns linked to it.

The Central Government has been given several authorities under this Act. According to the act's provisions, the Central Government has complete authority to enact any laws connected to international commerce in order to achieve the act's goals. This Act also gives the government the authority to enact any laws related to the formation of national import and export policy. The Act also allows the Central Government to designate a Director General by informing the appointment in the Official Gazette, and for the Director General to carry out all foreign trade policies in accordance with the rules.

THE ACT'S MOST IMPORTANT FEATURES

"The Foreign Trade (Development and Regulation) Act of 1992" is widely regarded as a watershed moment in the country's economic development, particularly in nowadays environment of industrialization as well as globalization. The whole legislation has been written in a way that it will operate in accordance with the existing trade policies of other nations.

Overall, this Act contains everything that strengthens the country's economy when overseas commerce is considered.

The following are regarded to be the act's most important features:

- The act gives the Central Government the authority to create laws for the growth and control of international commerce, including facilitating imports into the nation and increasing exports out of it, as well as any other subjects pertaining to international commerce.
- This legislation empowers the government to develop and declare export and import policies, as well as to alter them on a regular basis. The government also has broad authority to ban, restrict, and control exports and imports in general, as well as specific situations of international commerce.
- Many appointments, including that of the Director General, are made under the act to advise and assist the Central Government in the formulation and implementation of import and export policies.
- Every importer and exporter must receive an "Importer Exporter Code Number (IEC)" from the Director General or alawful person, according to the statute.

- The legislation ensures that all financial objectives in terms of imports and exports are met, allowing the country to attain its full economic potential. The key destinations here incorporate the help of support development concerning the fares of the country, the circulation of value labor and products to the homegrown buyer at universally cutthroat costs, incitement of supported monetary development by giving admittance to fundamental crude materials just as an upgrade of innovative strength and productivity of Indian horticulture, industry just as administrations and improvement of their seriousness to meet a wide range of prerequisite of the worldwide business sectors.

FOREIGN TRADE POLICY'S IMPORTANCE

Any country's foreign trade strategy is critical for the free movement of goods and services as well as the country's overall economic development. Any country that does not have a competent international trade strategy would struggle to run its import and export operations properly. If a country does not have a suitable foreign policy, the country's whole import-export and international commerce would fail horribly and will inevitably come to a halt. Any country's foreign trade policy enables a free flow of commerce and economic activity while dealing or dealing on a global scale. The same strategy contributes to the country's economy flowing freely, speeding financial growth, promoting free trade and liberalization, and raising the general standard of living for its citizens.

THE CURRENT STATE OF FOREIGN TRADE POLICY

India was set to launch its Foreign Trade Policy 2021-2026 on April 1. Due to Covid-19, which was set to cease on March 31, the previous policy was prolonged for another year. The administration chose to prolong it for another six months. The present policy will remain in effect until September 30th. The government's foreign trade policy (FTP) specifies plans and actions to encourage local production and exports with the goal of boosting economic growth."According to the United Nations' World Economic Situation and Prospects 2021 report, India's economy fell 9.6% in 2020, compared to a world average of 4.3 percent."[ii] India is expected to expand at 7.3 percent in 2021, according to the report. Exporters anticipate that the new policy will feature steps targeted at boosting India's position in global goods and services exports, as well as addressing the shortcomings of the Foreign Trade Policy 2015-2020.

International trade was severely harmed by Covid-19. In April 2020, India's exports decreased by a record 60 percent, while imports plummeted by 59 percent. Despite the fact that the situation has improved, the path to recovery remains lengthy and difficult. As a result, the new trade strategy must deliver on its promises.

<u>CONCLUSION</u>

Following the execution of India's international trade strategy, both import and export to other nations have expanded, and both have become quite safe and secure to carry out. "The Foreign Trade Policy of India" has expanded the total number of foreign investors in the nation by establishing several plans/policies such as SEZ and EPZ. Trading Housing has provided a platform for both consumers and producers, allowing for the simple exchange of goods between nations.

Besides, the streamlining of processes, as well as the concept of providing enticements to exporters and traders participating in international commerce, has functioned fairly for the merchants, albeit there is still room for improvement.

As a result of the establishment of the "Foreign Trade (Development and Regulation) Act, 1992" in India, industrialization has become more liberal, which has confirmed to be immensely advantageous for all merchants and customers in the future.

<u>Author's Bio</u>

A Passionate Law Student with excellent oral and written communication skills and an aim to make a difference through the power of words.

CHAPTER ELEVEN

JUDICIAL INTERVENTION IN ARBITRAL PROCESS; ANALYSIS OF BALCO V KAISER ALLUMINIUM JUDGEMENT

Author: Shivangi Sharma, III year of B.A.,LL.B.(Hons.) from Amity University Noida

ABSTRACT

One of the key purposes of the 1996 act was to provide the arbitrator more power while still allowing the parties more autonomy. Furthermore, the scope of legal action should be constrained. Although, in most cases, the Court of a different Judicial Authority does not intervene in any arbitration hearing or award. The non-intervention rule is based on the notion that once the parties to a commercial settlement have agreed to resolve their problems through mediation, conciliation, or arbitration, the legal system may no longer be justified in intervening with the arbitration proceeding. The courts, on the other hand, have the power to hear any dispute in which they feel the parties have failed to enter into a legitimate arbitration agreement. The question of whether Indian courts have the ability to overturn foreign arbitral decisions has the potential to have a major impact on the international arbitration community as well as international business in India.

The Indian Arbitration Act of 1996 covers the legal aspects of domestic arbitration, international commercial arbitration, and the enforcement of foreign arbitral judgments. Indian courts have used provisions of the Act to ignore contradictory contractual terms and establish their own authority in order to enact temporary measures and set aside arbitral judgments. . Foreign investors in India's construction, energy, and other industries have long been concerned about the Indian judiciary's proclivity to intervene in international arbitration processes. In Bharat Aluminium Co. v Kaiser Aluminium Technical Services, Inc., India's Supreme Court rejected previous judgments that authorized this interventionist policy, which is a positive move. The purpose of this article is to examine the jurisdiction of judicial intervention prior to and after the BALCO case.

Keywords- Judicial intervention, foreign award, BALCO, Relaince Industries and Bhatia International.

Introduction

People in India are becoming more reliant on alternative conflict resolution mechanisms as a result of the enormous number of cases standing before the Indian judiciary. Out-of-court settlement methods are the most practical means of ensuring rapid redress of disputes while avoiding unwarranted delays in the courts. As a result of arbitration's rapid growth, several roadblocks have emerged in its route to successfully delivering justice. Due to flaws in the legislative provisions, the judiciary is frequently seen as having to intervene during arbitration processes.[1]

Three key cases resulted in opposing views on the jurisdiction of Indian courts over international arbitrations. Bhatia International v. Bulk Trading S.A. and Anr.[2] was a high-profile case in which an Indian court was given the power to overturn the foreign awards. Bharat Aluminum Company v. Kaiser Aluminum Technical Services Inc. BALCO, concluded after ten years, overruled Bhatia Foreign and declared that Part I of the Act could not be invoked to grant Indian court's jurisdiction over international arbitrations. The BALCO court's decision was designed to clarify the situation, but it only applied to arbitration agreements filed after September 6, 2012. In Union of India vs. Reliance Industries Ltd & Anr[3], the court revisited BALCO, reinvigorating the Bhatia International judgment with respect to arbitration agreements executed before September 6, 2012.

As a result, Reliance Industries and BALCO devised two contradictory rules that apply solely to the date on which the parties agreed to the applicable arbitral clauses:

1. Broad application of Part I for arbitral agreements made before September 6, 2012; and
2. More restricted application of Part I for agreements made after September 6, 2012.

The ultimate focus of this paper is to analyse the Indian courts' lack of clarity on the subject of whether Indian courts have jurisdiction over contracts that assign jurisdiction to another country, and how this impacts international arbitration. India has recently developed a pro-arbitration jurisprudence that favours arbitration agreements that delegate jurisdiction to another country. Bhatia International and Reliance Industries, on the other hand, challenge that reputation and put the international arbitration community in India at risk of having unenforceable arbitration agreements. Following the court's decision in BALCO, the international arbitration community was adamant that they would no longer have to fear Indian courts establishing jurisdiction over their disputes governed by foreign law. The law's applicability, however, is limited.

Judicial Intervention

One of the main purposes of the 1996 Act was to provide arbitrators additional power while limiting the function of the court as a supervisor in the arbitration process. In practise, the 1996 Act allows for court involvement on a regular basis. For example, the term 'public policy' appears twice in the 1996 Act. Section 34 of the 1996 Act allows an award to be set aside if it is in conflict with Indian public policy (Part I). Furthermore, under Section 48 of the 1996 Act, if a foreign award is harmful to India's public policy, it may be denied for enforcement (Part II). Renusagar Power Electric Co v. General Electric Co[4], a case involving the execution of an ICC Judgement, the issue of public policy was raised for the first time as an exception for the enforcement of a foreign arbitral award.

The Arbitration and Conciliation Act 1996 consist of international commercial arbitration in India. Part I of the Arbitration Act provides a structure of rules for domestic arbitrations, which are any arbitrations held in India, including those involving a foreign party; and Part II provides rules for the recognition and enforcement of foreign arbitral awards, which are those issued by arbitrations held outside India, whether or not an Indian party is involved. The Arbitration Act closely resembles the UNCITRAL Model Law on International Commercial Arbitration, which proposes a legal framework for international arbitration that respects party autonomy and limits the extent to which local courts may intervene in the arbitral process, particularly in relation to international commercial arbitration.

However, the Indian courts have significantly weakened this principle of non-intervention in a series of cases. In Bhatia International v Bulk Trading S.A, the Supreme Court found that Part I of the Arbitration Act applied equally to arbitrations performed outside India, requiring higher degrees of court participation. In another case, the Court ruled that any foreign arbitral award that violated Indian law was invalid and liable to be overturned on public policy grounds.

The total result of these decisions was that Indian courts had the authority to reopen and examine any foreign arbitral award, whether seated in India or not, and whether or not a party wantt to enforce that foreign award in India. Because of this method, parties who had agreed to resolve their problems through arbitration, for example, Singapore could be dragged into legal proceedings in India before any attempt at local enforcement was undertaken. This strategy had caused considerable concern among foreign parties involved in economic transactions in India, as well as major criticism from Indian and international lawyers and academics.

Expansion of Jurisdiction over Foreign Awards

The case law underpinning the Indian courts' enlargement of jurisdiction over foreign arbitral panels is based on Bhatia International. Despite appearing to pertain primarily to domestic arbitrations, the Bhatia International court determined that Part I applied to international arbitrations. Eventually, the Bhatia International court found that Part I extended to international arbitrations unless the parties specifically or implicitly rejected it.

According to Bhatia International, Indian courts have the option of intervening in a foreign award as if it were an Indian award. When a dispute involving an Indian party arose, Bhatia International gave courts the authority to assert jurisdiction over international arbitration agreements and to set aside arbitral decisions rendered by foreign-seated panels. The court also stated that the agreement's non obstante clause trumps 'the totality of the agreement,' including the arbitration provision that provided that foreign law would rule. The non-obstante clause, which states that the parties will not violate Indian law, was proof of the parties purpose to have Indian law control their agreement, according to the court. As a result, the court gave the non obstante clause more weight than the contract terms that specified which law the parties agreed to apply to their deal.

Later instances, such as Venture Global Engineering v. Satyam Computer Systems Ltd. , demonstrated this strength. Venture Global and Satyam Computer had a Shareholder Agreement that included an arbitration clause. Satyam Computer filed a claim in the London Court of International Arbitration, stating that it was entitled to shares in a corporation controlled jointly by the parties as a result of Venture Global's claimed default. Satyam Computer sought enforcement in the United States District Court for the Eastern District of Michigan after the arbitrator found in its favour. Meanwhile, Venture Global filed a request in Indian court for an injunction and for the award to be set aside. The court in Venture Global used Part I to determine whether it had jurisdiction over the disputed contract. The Venture Global court was granted jurisdiction because the parties' agreement violated various Indian statutes and was contrary to Indian public policy.

The Venture Global case has far-reaching implications since it establishes a new mechanism and foundation for challenging a foreign award that the Act does not address. A person seeking to enforce a foreign award must now file both an application for enforcement under Section 48 of the Act and an application to set aside the award under Section 34 of the Act. The award must now pass not only the New York Convention grounds contained in Section 48 but also the extended 'public policy' basis introduced under Section 34 of the Act.

<u>Analysis of BALCO Judgement</u>

This decision has resolved a conflicting position that existed in relation to arbitration proceedings held outside India or international commercial arbitration with a seat of arbitration outside India, in which Indian parties sought the intervention of an Indian court to set aside foreign awards and render them unenforceable in India, thereby rendering the entire arbitration process futile.On September 6, 2012, the Supreme Court of India's Constitutional bench overruled its earlier decisions in Bhatia Trading v. Bulk Trading and Venture Global Engineering v. Satyam Computer Services Ltd, holding that Indian courts lack jurisdiction to interfere with foreign awards made in International Commercial Arbitration. The Supreme Court concluded that Part I of the Indian Arbitration and Conciliation Act, 1996 does not apply to arbitration proceedings occurring outside India and that an Indian court cannot use Part I of the Act to issue interim orders or set aside foreign decisions.

Videocon Industries Limited v. Union of India was one of the first cases to shift towards a more arbitration-friendly judiciary. According to the Videocon court, the lower court lacks jurisdiction because the parties agreed that any arbitration procedures would be controlled by English law. When the parties consented to have their conflicts governed by a non-Indian country's law, the court in Videocon's ruling indicated that the court was inclined to allow implied exclusions of Part I. In essence, Videocon demonstrated that Indian courts were willing to recognize the conflicting provisions that barred them from exercising jurisdiction over foreign arbitration agreements that did not follow Indian law. As a result, Videocon differed from Bhatia International and Venture Global's anti-arbitration determinations. Furthermore, Videocon paved the way for the future BALCO decision to clarify and expand on the acceptance of implied Part I exclusions.

In BALCO, the court considered whether the parties directly or implicitly excluded Part I from the court's jurisdiction over the matter. We are of the considered judgment that Part I of the Arbitration Act, 1996 would have no application to International Commercial Arbitration held outside India,' the court said. As a result, such awards will be subject to the jurisdiction of Indian courts only if they are sought to be implemented in India in conformity with the requirements of Part II of the Arbitration Act, 1996.The provisions of the Arbitration Act, 1996, in Court opinion, make it crystal plain that there can be no overlapping or intermingling of the provisions of Part I with the provisions of Part II of the Act. With all due respect, we cannot concur with the decisions reached by this Court in the Bhatia International and Venture Global Engineering cases.

The recognition that the law of the nation chosen as the seat of arbitration would apply to the arbitral proceedings is inextricably linked to the choice of that country as the seat of arbitration. The terms 'seat' and 'place' of arbitration are interchangeable, although the seat must remain the location specified in the arbitration agreement. International business arbitration involves parties from many countries, therefore the location of the arbitration may change, but the seat will remain the same. Section 48 of Part II does not give two courts the authority to annul the judgment; it is only included to give parties an opportunity to contest the award if the legislation of the nation where the arbitration is held lacks such a provision.The words 'set aside or suspend' in section 48 do not imply that the foreign award sought to be enforced can be challenged on the merits by

Indian courts; rather, the provision merely recognizes two nations courts as competent to suspend or annul the award and does not imply that the two courts have any jurisdiction to annul the award made outside India. The Indian Arbitration Act of 1996 does not expressly grant an Indian court the authority to set aside awards made outside of India.

Non-convention arbitral awards are not covered by Part I of the Act. Because the definition of foreign awards has been purposefully limited to the New York and Geneva conventions, there is no provision in the Act for the enforcement of non-convention arbitral awards, and thus no remedy can be incorporated in the Act; this can only be done by necessary amendments that can be introduced only by Parliament.The territoriality element of the Model Law has been incorporated in the Indian Arbitration Act of 1996. All sections of Part I [Section 1, 2 (4), (5), (7)] reaffirm that Part I applies to all arbitration procedures held in India and cannot be extended to international commercial arbitrations undertaken outside India on the basis of interpretation.

The BALCO court limited its judgement to just agreements entered into after September 6, 2012, when it was issued. As a result, the restriction on agreements taken into after BALCO left the door open to what the position would be on pre-BALCO agreements.The principles established in the stated judgment would be applied to arbitration agreements entered into on or after September 7, 2012. Although it may not appear to be a major issue at first glance, parties who signed arbitration agreements on or before September 6, 2012, providing for foreign seated international commercial arbitrations, would be required to repeat the time-consuming process of reviewing all such arguments in light of the BALCO Case rulings and amending the agreements, if necessary, to avoid any ambiguity.

Some Problems Related to BALCO Judgement-

Despite the fact that there are other challenges that need to be addressed by Indian courts in the wake of the BALCO decision, the BALCO ruling offers the essential motivation for Indian courts to get off to a solid start. This absence of interim remedies under the Act could be particularly harmful to the arbitral process in such foreign seated arbitrations where the subject matter of the dispute is located in India. Even if a favourable award is made, the purpose of the arbitration proceedings may be defeated because the party against whom the award is made, if it has assets in India, can dispose of those assets during the pendency of the arbitration in order to defeat any award made against such party outside India.

Despite the fact that Bhatia and Venture Global have been expressly overruled, the BALCO decision essentially indicates that these precedents are unlikely to continue to be a precedent for any judgement by an Indian court relating to arbitration agreements made before September 6, 2012. Given the preceding decisions, it is clear that the BALCO decision is not the panacea for all of India's arbitration woes, but it has clearly demonstrated that the Supreme Court has taken a step in the right way.

Post BALCO Judgement

It was unclear after the BALCO judgment what rule would apply to arbitration agreements signed before September 6, 2012. Union of India v. Reliance Industries addressed this issue.

The Reliance Industries dispute stemmed from two Production Sharing Contracts ("PSCs") involving the exploration and production of petroleum from India's Tapti and Panna Muleta areas. The contracts were signed in 1994 and were meant to last for 25 years unless the parties agreed otherwise. Reliance submitted a variety of claims, including royalties, cesses, and service taxes. The Union of India objected, claiming that the claims were unresolvable through arbitration. Despite this, the arbitral tribunal found Reliance's claims to be arbitrable.As a result, the Union of India filed a claim in the Delhi High Court to have the arbitral decision set aside under Part I, Section 34. Reliance objected, claiming that the arbitration agreement in the PSCs stipulated that English law would govern and that any disputes would be handled by a London-based arbitration panel.

The fundamental question before the Reliance Industries court was whether the parties specifically or implicitly excluded Part I. Rather than finding the parties had excluded Part I, Indian courts, such as the Venture Global court, had previously relied on public policy issues to justify their jurisdiction. The Indian court's authority was also linked to public policy considerations arising from Indian objects, taxes, and government involvement in the PSCs, according to the Reliance Industries court.

When there is a non obstante clause prohibiting the parties from breaching Indian laws, the Reliance Industries court concluded: No inference as to exclusion of the jurisdiction of Indian courts can be made by this court because it seems that the parties' intent is not to exclude Indian laws, and the court has the jurisdiction.

Because the holding in BALCO only applied to agreements made after the judgment was handed down in 2012, whereas the arrangement between

Reliance Industries and the Union of India was signed in 1994, the Reliance Industries decision followed Venture Global rather than BALCO. When the Reliance Industries court applied Bhatia International and Venture Global to this case, the court found no evidence that the parties omitted Part I. As a result, Reliance's objection to the court's jurisdiction over the parties' agreement was overruled.

Following the 2015 amendment to the Arbitration and Conciliation Act, Indian courts have moved away from their usual methodological analysis of minor intervention in cases involving the requirement of foreign awards, and have taken significant steps to prevent enforcement solely on the basis of strained grounds.

The courts have gone about giving impetus in the enforcement of foreign awards in the manner in which the prevailing legislation on the enforcement of foreign awards has been dependent entirely on these modifications in the BALCO and the subsequent in the 2015 Amendment has made India an Arbitration centre. While there will still be a long and arduous road ahead, fraught with legal and policy obstacles in terms of applicability and jurisdiction.

<u>Conclusion</u>

Changes that occurred after the BALCO Decision: This was a significant advance in the field because it constituted a paradigm shift from past practise. The Supreme Court's readiness to do so sent a message to Indian courts that they will not be afraid to follow the terms of applicable international accords and align Indian legislation with an equivalent. This is significant because one of the major challenges that arbitration practitioners in India face is that the courts must adjust to arbitration processes controlled by a statute based on the UNCITRAL Model Law. Foreign investors, on the other hand, gained fresh confidence in dealing with Indian parties as a result of this.By adopting the rationale from Venture Global, Reliance Industries increased the power of Indian courts to exercise jurisdiction over foreign commercial arbitrations. Despite BALCO overruling both Bhatia Foreign and Venture Global by holding that Indian courts could no longer exercise jurisdiction over international arbitration agreements entered into after September 6, 2012, Reliance Industries has returned to this old line of thought. Because of the court's ruling in Reliance Industries, Indian courts are once again free to exercise jurisdiction over internal commercial arbitrations where the parties have chosen to have their issues governed by foreign law.

These two contradictory techniques are incompatible and should not coexist. Until the Court definitively overrules either BALCO or Bhatia Foreign and Reliance Industries, the issue of Indian courts having jurisdiction over international arbitrations would remain unsettled. When these hurdles are overcome, India may really be termed an arbitration-friendly nation, which the BALCO judgment has already imbued with a new light of optimism that a new and promising age for arbitral proceedings in India has begun.

CHAPTER TWELVE

SHOULD LEGISLATURE CRIMINALIZE MARITAL RAPE

Author: Mihir Chandra, II year of B.A.,LL.B. from Babu Banarasi Das University, Lucknow

During the evolution of democracy there are now more lenient laws which are evolving and that should have the first priority to safe guard the personal rights and dignity of individual. From beginning women continuously faces violence and cruelty no doubt. During the past time colonial period, women have not their personal rights and was chattel under their husband or in the society. From the past till the present many laws have been evolved and if I talked about India then there are many.

But the air is now filled with the talks about marital rape. How this is even a rape? How we consider it as a rape?

Generally while having sexual intercourse the word consent matters and also there is age restriction. For example if a man tries to intercourse with the minor who is below 18 even by her consent then that will amount of rape and that person shall be booked under IPC 375.

Now the question is if the consent was not given by wife and if the husband forcefully try to sex with his wife then this will not amount to rape but if a man tries to sex with unmarried women then there is the offence of rape, how this come fair?

If we dive down to the fact that many men are now afraid with this debate, the most probable cause are:-

1) **The concept of adultery**

What if the women engaged in extra marital affair with another men? According to IPC 497 Whoever has sexual intercourse with a person who is and whom he knows or has reason to believe to be the wife of another man, without the consent or connivance of that man, such sexual intercourse not amounting to the offence of rape, is guilty of the offence of adultery, and shall be punished with imprisonment of either description for a term which may extend to five years, or with fine, or with both. In such case, the wife shall not be punishable as an abettor.

Now in present days the adultery is not comes under crime and has no validity under IPC. I have specifically mentioned this because always men will held responsible under this offence and not the women.

2) The concept of divorce and maintenance

Now as we know that adultery is not a crime but we can use adultery as a ground for divorce with the help of certain personal laws in which the marriage had performed. But the question is what happen after divorce? The concept of maintenance arises after divorce and either party have to give an amount of money depending upon their condition the problem is that if one of them are engaged in extra affairs and also enjoys the maintenance then how this come fair? I know if anyone of them is successful for proving the adultery then no maintenance shall be provided but the point is someone have to prove and this is the most complex process.

3) The concept of saptpadi under Hindu law

Under this there is seven steps around the fire and many promises have been made to each other. From one of the promise there is one where female promise to her husband that she is titally ready with him in mental as well as physical condition after marriage. From here the defense against marital rape arises because the word consent matters when it comes to rape and in this the female already given her proper consent.

Now this is all about under the Hindu law but what about other laws? If we want a uniform civil code then there should be separate laws under this. We can not put this concept under the narrower sense because this debate itself connected with the right of gender and a small mistake will leads many problems in the personal life of the person.

<u>**Legal point of view**</u>

Article 14:- Equality before law and equal protection of law

It means that law must be equal to all person and if there is any discrimination than it must be reasonable and rational and total autonomy of husband over the body of wife is totally arbitrary, unreasonable and violates the basic principle of Article 14

Article 15: Article 15 says that there must not be any discrimination on the ground of sex and making the sexual relation against the consent of wife violates the Article 15

Article 15 (3): No laws can be against the women but explanation 2 of Article 375 make it clear that Husband can not be punished for the offence of Rape

Article 21: Everyone have the right to take a decision over their personal life and body and making the sexual intercourse against the consent of wife is against the Article 21 of Indian Constitution

In the sakhi v. Union of India Supreme Court held that explanation (2) of section 375 of Indian penal code should be deleted forced intercourse by a husband with his wife should be treated equally as an offence just as any physical violence by a husband against the wife is a treated as an offence

International law and marital Rape

In December 1993 the United State nations High commissioner for human right published the declaration on the elimination of violence against women .This establishes marital Rape as a human right violation . In 1997 UNICEF reported that just 17 states had criminalized marital Rape In 2003 UNIFEM reported that more than 50 states did so . The countries like Poland soviet union were first to criminalized marital Rape.

Recent countries to criminalise marital Rape include Zimbabwe (2001), Turkey, Cambodia (2005) Malaysia (2007) Thailand (2007) South Korea (2013). According to UN population fund more than two third of the married women in India. Aged between 15 to 49 are severely beaten or forced to provide sex

Ongoing debate views and argument under Delhi High court

The bench said, Is the firewall justifiable on the test of Articles 14 and 21? It is only that narrow aspect that we have to look into. To say that the wife can go and seek divorce if the husband imposes himself on her is not the issue here.

"Why is it so different from an unmarried woman? It affects an unmarried woman's dignity but it does not affect the dignity of a married woman? How is it? What is the answer to this? Does she lose her right to say 'no'? Have 50 countries (which have made marital rape an offence) got it wrong?

The bench did not appreciate the argument advanced by the Delhi government that a married woman has the remedy to divorce on the ground of cruelty under the personal laws and she can also register a criminal case against her husband under IPC section 498A (cruelty to married woman)

The exception to section 375 does not violate the admitted right to privacy, dignity or the right to refuse sex in or out of marriage because there is no compulsion on a woman and she is not remediless. While opposing the pleas to strike down the exception granted to husbands under the Indian rape law, the Delhi government counsel said the petitioners would have to show that this exemption compels a wife to cohabit with her husband and violates her dignity. The Delhi government counsel said if the court comes to a conclusion to strike down the exception, a new offence will have to be created and the constitutional scheme does not permit the judiciary to create a new offence as it does not have the machinery as that of the legislature.

This debate is still are going in the court and there is no any final decision but we have to give our opinion on this topic because the work of the law makers is to just made the laws by keeping all the sentiments of the society together but in personal life we have to face the consequences and there is no doubt if the problem arises then there is lot to take and half of life will get spoiled.

<u>Opinion</u>

In my point of view there should be law which should criminalise the marital rape and protect the right and dignity of the women as a whole. But there should be laws or there should be a proper direction for men also so that the rights for them are also protected because as evolving of many laws for women there is increase in false cases against men which itself make women as a immune entity against men.

No doubt women face many problems but in this modern democracy every persons rights are important and should be provided equally. Improvising many laws is not the solution, the solutionis to implement one law as whole and with full potential.

I would like to end my article with the quote:-

Democracy must be built through open societies that share information. When there is information, there is enlightenment. When there is debate, there are solutions. When there is no sharing of power, no rule of law, no accountability, there is abuse, corruption, subjugation and indignation - Atifete Jahjaga

<u>Author's Bio</u>

Mihir chandra is a first year student at uttar predesh state of Babu Banarasi Das University, school of legal studies where he is pursuing BA

LLB. In his studies Mihir is focusing on Indian constitution and Indian penal code of 1860 including CRPC And CPC also he is furthering his knowledge of different acts in India and contract law of 1872. His interest in communication steam from his goal of communicating the importance of Human rights and its uses in India to the large audience. Upon completion of his undergraduate studies, he intends to apply for judicial service examination for different states and will serve the society with his full esteem.

CHAPTER THIRTEEN

COUNTRIES OF SOUTH ASIA AND THEIR ROLE IN THE WELFARE STATE

Author: Yashika Mor, pursuing B.A.,LL.B. from B.A.,LL.B. from Geeta Institute of Law

Despite the fact that Asian developmental welfare state models are still in their infancy, they may provide a useful baseline for the post-2015 development debate. The role of the state has diminished, and it needs to be reviewed in light of a new, comprehensive, and progressive »development« agenda beyond 2015, as well as rising disparities within and between countries. The welfare state – in the form of a democratic developmental welfare state – is an ideal framework for framing the issue for this purpose because of its commitment to both social fairness and democracy. The neoliberal goal of replacing government activities with the market and private sector is gaining traction. A well-functioning, accountable, and sufficiently resourced state is essential to address inequities. There are five basic types of developmental welfare states in Asia, each responding differently to poverty, vulnerability, social exclusion, demographic challenges, environmental stress, and, to a lesser extent, wealth disparities. Despite its claims to be committed to welfare state programmes, Asia has seen disparities in human development, poverty reduction, social income equality, and social inclusion spending. In terms of its commitment to social justice, the welfare state can be characterised as assuring universal access to social services, setting procedures for access to employment and decent work, and offering a package of social benefits.

The government assists individuals, provides social security, and enforces environmental standards, among other things. In this context, social protection functions as both a mechanism for income redistribution (through tax policy mechanics) and a source of long-term systemic stability. Due to the increasing intensity of vulnerability, income and multidimensional poverty, employment informality, income inequality, and ecological degradation observed in all countries, the potential for income redistribution and environmental regulation has become especially important in the current discourse on gender equality, social inclusion, and intergenerational justice. Social security is divided into two types: contribution-based and tax-funded. Environmental policy, defined as policies and actions that address environmental sustainability, has recently been seen as vital to welfare state policy (UNRISD 2014), and hence might be considered a sixth pillar in the enterprise sector. The list, obviously, reflects a broad view of the welfare state. Most countries play a welfare state role, according to a liberal interpretation of these requirements, with policies spanning education and health, social protection, labour market programmes, and family policy. Compulsory elementary education is currently the norm around the world, even if it is not free in many nations. Health-care delivery systems and health-insurance coverage are changing in a variety of ways. Many governments have attempted to make it safer and more affordable. At least 50 countries have implemented or enhanced social safety net programmes such as direct cash transfers and school lunches (United Nations 2013: 33)

The first is a set of developmental welfare states that intervened in the economy with a deliberate industrial policy aimed at increasing agricultural output, fostering new manufacturing branches, or easing the transition to the service sector. Initially, these countries undertook social endeavours to improve the lives of their residents. Two questions have been attempted to be answered in this short. One source of concern is the state's participation in the democratic (developmental) welfare state in its apparently progressive form. The second looks at the natural environment, examining the characteristics of Asian welfare states in order to determine whether an Asian welfare state mode exists. Five principles underpin SAARC cooperation: sovereign equality, territorial integrity, political independence, non-interference in member states' internal affairs, and mutual benefit. Bilateral and international ties between SAARC member countries are bolstered through regional cooperation. Every year, the SAARC Summit is held, and the country hosting the event serves as the Association's Chair. Decisions must be unanimous, and bilateral and contentious issues are not discussed in the SAARC. Nine Observer States attend SAARC Summits in addition to the eight Member States: China, the United States, Myanmar, Iran, Japan, South Korea, Australia, Mauritius, and the European Union.

With about 1 billion people living under democratic regimes, South Asia is the world's most populated region among constitutional democratic republics, compared to populations of 500 million in the European Union, North America, and South America. Bangladesh, India, and Pakistan, the three main countries of the Indian subcontinent, began their modern democratic journey as members of the British Indian Empire, particularly with British India's parliament. In 1931, the Donoughmore Constitution gave Sri Lankans full suffrage, making it Asia's oldest democracy. Fundamental rights are now inscribed in the constitutions of every country in South Asia. SOUTH ASIA is a vast Asian region to the east of the Indian subcontinent and to the south of China. A continental projection (often known as mainland Southeast Asia) and a string of archipelagos to the south and east make up the region (insular Southeast Asia). Although the Malay Peninsula, which reaches 700 miles (1,100 kilometres) south into insular Southeast Asia, is nominally part of the mainland, it has significant natural and cultural ties to the surrounding islands, serving as a link between them.

CHAPTER FOURTEEN

EXAMINING SECTION 15 OF THE JUVENILE JUSTICE (CARE AND PROTECTION OF CHILDREN) ACT, 2015

Author: Prerna Deep, Law Clerk-cum-Research Assistant under Hon'ble Justice at the Supreme Court of India

"There can be no more intense discovery of a society's spirit than how it treats its youngsters."

-Nelson Mandela

Abstract

The preamble of the Juvenile Justice (Care and Protection of Children) Act, 2015 (herein now referred to as The Act of 2015) highlights that the primary objective of "the Act of 2015" is to serve in the best interest of children which includes but is not limited to safeguarding their basic rights and needs by catering to their physical, emotional, and intellectual development.

This article critically analyses one of the most debated provisions of the Juvenile Justice (Care and Protection of Children) Act, 2015, Section 15. The article provides a brief description of the provision, dissects the legal impediments and plausible challenges in implementing the provision, and concludes. Section 15 of "the Act of 2015" allows the trial of 16-18 years old children in the adult criminal court if they are alleged to have committed a heinous offence. To make an informed decision, the juvenile justice board has been bestowed upon the duties of determining the nature of crimes as heinous, the correct age of the juvenile offender in question, conducting requisite preliminary assessments, and finally deciding whether the juvenile needs to be transferred to the children's court. After further deliberation, the children's court decides if the alleged juvenile offender should be tried as an adult.

Introduction

A new era of juvenile justice has been spun by introducing The Juvenile Justice (Care and Protection of Children) Act, 2015 in the Indian Criminal Jurisprudence. The introduction of the present laws stems from the criticism regarding the inadequacy of the Juvenile Justice Act, 2000 to provide justice in its true sense. The lacunae in the Juvenile Justice Act, 2000 came to light when in 2012, the infamous Delhi gang rape and murder case[1] took place. One of the accused of the case was a juvenile who was given somewhat less punishment for his acts despite being the alleged primary accused. According to the provisions of the Juvenile Justice Act, 2000, he was sentenced to three years in a reformation home. The family of the victim and the people of India stood united, protesting against the provisions that gave the accused a nominal punishment of the gruesome and soul retching act he committed with the aid of other co-accused persons. It is an established principle of law that justice must not only be served but also be visible to be served which failed in this case. Consequently, the Juvenile Justice (Care and Protection of Children) Bill, 2014 was drafted, shaping the present law.

Legal Lacunae

The scope of 'heinous crimes' under "The Act of 2015" is vague[2]. It mentions crimes with a minimum of seven years or more imprisonment and is not exhaustive by incorporating terminology such as 'includes,' which allows encompassing various crimes under its domain that the children may not even be aware of. The provision contrasts with the statutory principles of "The Act of 2015", primarily of 'presumption of innocence' and 'principle of the best interest.' [3]

"The Act of 2015" fails to follow the basic tenets of law as enshrined under the Articles 14, 15(3), 21, 24, 39(e), 39(f), 45, and 47 Constitution of India, 1950. These provisions impose guidelines and obligations on the State for the protection of children and safeguarding their rights. The provisions are further in violation of Article 1 and General Comment 10 of the UN Convention on the Rights of the Child, 1989.

Gaps in Implementation

The initial timeline mentioned in the provision [4] to determine the suitability of transfer fails to consider the practicality. There is a lack of proper infrastructure, coordination between different stakeholders, delay in administrative work [5], and involvement of inaccurate tests such as bone ossification for age determination. [6] These pose significant threats to the decision regarding the transfer of the child to adult court. The stakeholders in the juvenile justice system are specially trained and sensitised[7], but once the case is transferred to the adult court, the juveniles are likely to face other unforeseen obstacles.

Conclusion

The laws pertaining to juveniles have taken centre stage in today's India. In the light of the above discussion and analysis, it is concluded that section 15 of "The Act of 2015" in its present form reeks of uncertainty, ambiguity and is inefficient in providing the juveniles the protection and safeguards they are entitled to in the law. In its current format, the studied provision of "The Act of 2015" needs reconsideration and redesigning.

Author's Bio

Prerna Deep is the recipient of British Council GREAT Scholarship (2019) for pursuing LLM in Criminal Law and Criminal Justice at the University of Edinburgh. She is currently working as a Law Clerk-cum-

Research-Assistant under Hon'ble Justice of Supreme Court of India. She holds LL.B. from Campus Law Centre, University of Delhi and English Honours from Miranda House, University of Delhi. As an avid reader and writer, Prerna has authored several Nationally and Internationally published research papers and articles.

CHAPTER FIFTEEN

GITHA HARIHARAN AND ANOTHER VS. RESERVE BANK OF INDIA AND ANOTHER, 1999

Author: Ritik Agrawal, III year of B.Com.,LL.B. from Institute of law Jiwaji University

Co-author: Nishtha, II year of B.A.,LL.B. from University of Allahabad

ABSTRACT

This research made an attempt to evaluate the well-known Githa Hariharan decision. We'll start by learning the fundamental principles behind notions like guardianship and parental responsibility. We'll examine how some laws are still based on patriarchal notions, and how this is harmful to society. The natural guardian's rights and responsibilities will be discussed. In this article, we will analyse how the court failed torecognise the underlying issue and relied on ratios from other cases to judge the case, which were not similar to the current one.

In both the Indian and English contexts, there will be some discussion of the rights available to a natural guardian as regards the minor's person. By the end, we will have shown how this judgement fails to address the gender imbalance in the statutes in question, and a few alternative approaches to dealing with difficulties comparable to those raised in this case will be given.

Keywords-AFTER constitution of india; gender justice; gender discrimination; judicial interpretation;

INTRODUCTION

A Guardian is someone who is responsible for the protection of a minor's person and possessions. There's a distinction to be made between custody and guardianship. Custody refers to the minor's day-to-day physical care, whereas guardianship refers to the minor's right to make crucial and major decisions about his life and property.

This case is significant because it established for the first time that a natural guardian, as defined by the HMGA, 1956, can be either a father or a mother: whoever is capable of and available for taking care of the child and is deeply interested in the child's welfare, regardless of whether or not that person is the father.

This is a watershed moment in Indian legal history when it comes to guardianship issues. This decision interpreted and established that the word "after" in Section 6(a) of the Hindu Marriage and Guardianship Act, 1956, does not mean that the mother is the guardian of the minor child only after the father's death; rather, it means that a natural guardian can be both a mother and a father, whoever cares for the child's welfare and is interested in the child's benefit.

Githa Hariharan v. Reserve Bank of India (1999 2 SCC 228), in this case court was deciding the constitutional validity of Sec 6 of Hindu Minority and Guardianship act. The challenge was based on discrimination with women as the father is considered natural guardian of the minor, not the woman.

BRIEF FACTS OF THE CASE

The case revolves around the mother's entitlement to be legally recognised as the son's natural guardian while the husband is away. The first petitioner, Ms Githa Hariharan, married DR. Mohan Ram in 1982. They had an unmarried child named Rishab Bailey in July of 1984. The petitioners jointly applied to the Reserve Bank of India (RBI) in December 1984 for a Rs. 20,000 9 percent Relief Bond to be held in the name of her minor son. The petitioner, as the child's mother, applied to be the minor's natural guardian in connection to the administration of funds held in her son's name for investment reasons.

The Reserve Bank of India rejected Ms. Githa Hariharan's application, requesting that the couple either present an application form with the child's father listed as the domestic guardian or a certificate from a competent body confirming the mother's guardianship.

Ms. Githa Hariharan responded by filing a writ petition seeking to have Section 6(a) of the Hindu Minority and Guardianship Act (HMG), 1956 and Section 19(b) of the Guardian and Wards Act (GW), 1890 declared unconstitutional on the grounds that they violate Articles 14 and 15 of the Indian Constitution. Because she entered the identical plea in her divorce case, the court combined the two cases and heard them simultaneously.

<u>**ISSUES OF THE CASE**</u>

1. Is it legal for a minor's mother to be recognised as her natural guardian?

2. Whether a mother has an equal guardianship right over the minor as the father?

3. Violation of the right to equality guaranteed under Articles 14 and 15 of the Indian Constitution and Prohibition of Discrimination guaranteed under Article 14 and Article 15 of the Indian Constitution

Guardianship in the Dark Ages We should delve at the origins of current guardianship laws before analysing various rules in modern-day India. India's guardianship laws are strongly influenced by English common law and colonial laws from pre-independence India. These laws reflect society's patriarchal and gendered values. Even if custody is shared, the father is ideally suited to have sole guardianship of his children. This was due to the patriarchal belief that males have a greater understanding of the outside world and are more able to make judgments about property and children's education. The father's right to guardianship was deemed absolute. We must remember these gendered beginnings in order torecognise the reforms in the legislation that have been made to include the rights of child.

<u>**ARGUMENTS FROM THE PETITIONER SIDE**</u>

The constitutional validity of the provision mentioned in section 6 (a) of the Hindu Minority and Guardianship Act, 1956 was challenged in the Supreme Court on the grounds that it violated Article 14 and Article 15 of the Indian Constitution, which guarantee the right to equality and prohibition of discrimination.

The petitioner claimed that the Reserve Bank of India's disclosure was arbitrary and in violation of the Indian Constitution's basic principle of fairness. As a result, the legitimacy of Section 6 (a) of the Hindu Minority and Guardianship Act, 1956 is being questioned. It was also claimed that the provision is discriminatory in nature, putting women at a disadvantage in child-related affairs. Acts that severely disadvantage women and discriminate against them when it comes to guardianship rights, obligations, and power over their own children.

<u>**ARGUMENTS FROM THE RESPONDENT SIDE**</u>

The bank's claim was based on Section 6(a) of the HMG Act, which states:

"The natural guardians of a Hindu minor, in respect of the minor's person as well as his or her property (excluding his or her undivided interest in joint family property), are- in the case of a boy or an unmarried girl-the father, and after him, the mother: provided that custody of a minor under the age of five years shall ordinarily be with the mother;"

It cannot be denied that, at the time, the accurate meaning of this clause was that a mother could not be a natural guardian of a minor in the presence of the father.

Who is a Natural Guardian

Section 6 of the Hindu Minority and Guardianship Act talks about the natural guardian.

1. The father is the natural guardian of a boy and an unmarried girl. After him, the mother becomes the natural guardian of the child.

2. The custody of the child who is five years old or has not completed the age of five shall be with the mother.

3. The mother is a natural guardian of the child who is illegitimate, whether a boy or an unmarried girl.

4. The husband is considered to be the natural guardian of a married girl.

5. If the child is adopted son, then the natural guardian is the adoptive father and after him, the adoptive mother.[1]

LEGAL ASPECTS

• Section 6 of the Hindu Minority and Guardianship Act 1956 (The natural guardians of a Hindu minor, in respect of the minor's person as well as in respect of the minor's property (excluding his or her undivided interest in joint family property), are ... in the case of a boy or an unmarried girl-the father, and after him, the mother: provided that the custody of a minor who has not completed the age of five years shall ordinarily be with the mother) [2]

• Guardian Constitution and Wards Act 1879

• Constitution of India, Article 14 (Equality before the law) and Article 15 (prohibition of discrimination on grounds of religion, race, caste, sex or place of birth)[3]

THE JUDGEMENT

Section 6. Natural Guardian: The natural guardians of a Hindu, minor, in respect of the minor's person as well as in respect of the minor's property (excluding his or her undivided interest in joint family property), are – (a) in the case of a boy or an unmarried girl—the father, and after him, the mother: provided that the custody of a minor who has not completed the age of five years shall ordinarily be with the mother; (b) in the case of an illegitimate boy or an illegitimate unmarried girl – the mother, and after her, the father; (c) in the case of a married girl – the husband.[4]

The constitutional validity of the provision mentioned in section 6 (a) of the Hindu Minority and Guardianship Act, 1956 was challenged in the Supreme Court on grounds that the above-stated provision violated the Right to Equality and Prohibition of Discrimination guaranteed under Article 14 and Article 15 of the Indian Constitution.[5]

The petitioner argued that the disclosure from the Reserve Bank of India was arbitrary and opposed to the basic concept of justice given in the Constitution of India. Thereby, challenging the validity of Section 6 (a) of the Hindu Minority and Guardianship Act, 1956. It was also argued that the provision is discriminatory in nature and keeps women at disadvantage concerning matters related to their children.[6]

Banerjee J, writing for the Court, emphasised the importance of the child's welfare over all other concerns. He addressed the case of Gajre v. Pathankhan (1970 2 SCC 717) in which, despite the fact that the father was alive, he showed no interest in the child's circumstances. The mother was found to be the natural guardian of her minor daughter in that case. He stated that, according to Hindu law and the Act, the father is the natural guardian, followed by the mother, but that this was not the case in the above situation.

The judgment in Gajre v Pathankhan considered that: "... a rigid insistence of strict statutory interpretation may not be conducive for the growth of the child, and welfare being the predominant criteria, it would be a plain exercise of judicial power of interpreting the law so as to be otherwise conducive to a fuller and better development and growth of the child." Justice Banerjee noted that the judge in Gajre v. Pathankhan allowed the mother to be the natural guardian: "... but without expression of any opinion as regards the true and correct interpretation of the word 'after' or deciding the issue as to the constitutionality of the provision as contained in Section 6(a) of the Act of 1956." He felt strongly that a long-established law should not easily be set aside; that a key point was interpretation of the word "after"; and that: "... the word did not necessarily mean after the death of the father, on the contrary, it [means] 'in the absence off' be it temporary or otherwise or total apathy of the father towards the child or even inability of the father by reason of ailment or otherwise."

He concluded that ascribing the literal meaning to the word 'after' cannot arise having due regard to the object of the Act and the constitutional guarantee of gender equality, since any other interpretation would render the statute void which ought to be avoided.

He then dismissed the petition challenging the Act's constitutionality, but urged the Reserve Bank to develop adequate methodologyin light of his findings. He also told the Delhi District Court to consider his opinions when deciding on the minor child's custody and guardianship.

The Court observed in para 9 says, "Is that the correct way of understanding the section and does the word 'after' in the section only mean 'after the lifetime'? If this question is answered in the affirmative, the section has to be struck down as unconstitutional as it undoubtedly violates gender equality, one of the basic principles of our Constitution.

The HMG Act came into force in 1956, i.e., six years after the Constitution. Did the Parliament intend to transgress the Constitutional limits and ignore the fundamental rights guaranteed by the Constitution which essentially prohibits discrimination on the grounds of sex.

<u>CONCLUSION</u>

Guardianship is a crucial and delicate area of family law. The welfare of the minor should be the most important concern when deciding on guardianship. It's all about the child's well-being. In India, guardianship rules have a shady history dating back to common law and colonial periods. Since then, India has embraced a forward-thinking stance. However, major obstacles to a child's best interests still exist. Patriarchal concepts of natural guardianship and stringent religious grounds are among them. Mother or someone else becomes a guardian only if the father is incompetent to be a natural guardian.

We may learn from the facts, issues, and the Supreme Court's ruling that fighting for our rights is an important part of our lives. The judicial review power, which has been bestowed in the court, must be exercised appropriately and without creating any overrules. Simply declaring any provision of an Act illegal or void is not the proper method of judicial review; instead, determining the intent of the provision in question is an important aspect of determining the constitutionality of any Act. The judiciary plays its duty in the aforesaid matter in a proper and perfect manner, as evidenced by the decision.

CHAPTER SIXTEEN

ANALYSIS OF UNREGULATED DIGITAL LENDING AND THE WAY FORWARD

Author: Arpit Jhanwar, IV year of B.A.,LL.B.(Hons.) from Symbiosis Law School, Pune

Introduction

The increased use of technology in the financial sector to provide hassle-free services such as lending has encouraged entities such as Nonbanking Financial Companies ("NBFCs") to collaborate with digital lending platforms ("DLPs") in order to reach out to their customers..[1] Over the years the NBFC sector has gone through various highs and lows to achieved systemic importance due to their interlinkage with banks, capital market and diverse portfolio of services. They have evolved their business model in terms of the growing economy and evolving regulatory milieu. [2]

Under NBFCs portfolio, lending through DLP segment is struggling over the past few years and a lot of negative factors have come to light including incidents of suicides[3] amongst those who failed to repay loans taken digitally through mobile apps. The cause of these incidents includes high-handed methods of recovery and use of personal information. This has brought concerns surrounding digital lending under the radar of the Reserve Bank of India (RBI). RBI strengthened its regulatory oversight over the sector and issued norms to ensure that the DLPs and NBFCs strictly comply with the Fair Practices Code and Outsourcing Guidelines[4]. Currently, it has set up a working group[5] to recommend a framework to regulate the digital lending industry.

In this article, I will examine the regulatory gaps that allowed lending apps to take up such exploitative practices in the first place. Further, I will analyze the existing guidelines and finally, I will explore the way forward to prevent these incidents.

Research Question

- Existing regulatory vacuum- narrow scope of regulatory framework or lack of enforcement mechanism?
- What is the impact and effectiveness of RBI issued norms ensuing strict and additional compliance with the Fair Practices Code and Outsourcing Guidelines?
- What is the way forward?

Hypothesis

It is evident from the evidence available on record that unregulated lending has created havoc in the masses mostly the informal sector. This can be clearly attributed to either narrow scope of regulatory framework or lack of enforcement. The author is of the view that both of these factors are equally responsible.

Furthermore, the RBI has taken a cognizance of the lack of regulatory framework and issue particular guidelines in that regards. Even after these guidelines the unregulated lending is rampant across India. Taking this as premise the author will further look into the possible way forward to regulate the lending market as the RBI itself is in the process of releasing a working committee report aimed to strengthen the regulatory framework.

Scope and Objective

Scope

This article focuses on the online based and mobile app based lending by NBFCs through DLPs and DLPs working independently. As such it makes use of existing rules and guidelines issued by RBI and various state governments to analyze the regulatory gap or lack of enforcement.

This is a comprehensive article with India as its geographic area of research and unregulated lending as its area of focus. The author has taken a problem-based approach to study into the existing regulatory gap, analyzing the effectiveness of proposed or currently implemented solutions by RBI. Finally, proposing a new solution to enhance the overall efficiency of the sector.

Objective

The primary objective of this research is to determine the existing regulatory gap and lack of implementation. Followed by, looking into the impact and effectiveness of newly proposed or upcoming regulations. Finally, proposing a way forward to deal with the issue of unregulated lending. The secondary objective includes identifying the modus operandi of these lending apps and the quantum at which they operate.

Chapter I - Existing regulatory vacuum- narrow scope of regulatory framework or lack of enforcement mechanism?

Online platform based and digital lending apps, which acts as bridge between the consumers and the financial institutions, have to be registered with banks or NBFCs. These intermediaries or facilitators have to follow and strictly adhere to the "Fair Practice Code"[6] (FPC) as envisaged by the RBI, both in form and substance (A detailed analysis of the FPC will be taken up in Chapter II). While going through the FPC it must be noted that the same applies to those DLPs which are linked to NCFCs or banks. Hence, DLPs whose money lending source does not arise from public deposit are outside its purview. These Apps are basically governed by specific Money lending statues of respective states.

The RBI has received complaint against 1,509 digital lending apps out of which 1,019 are unregulated or unregistered and 490 are registered NBFCs engaged in the business of digital lending.[7] Taking a note of the same, it is imperative to look into the existing legislative frame work.

RBI Guidelines[8]

- Except as stipulated in the terms and circumstances of the loan sanction agreements, lenders shall refrain from interfering in the affairs of borrowers.
- In case of recovery of loans, no resort should be made to undue harassment

State Lending Statue

- In General- imposes a requirement of obtaining license and the same is sanctioned after making a security deposit based on the money being invested in the lending activity. This ensures that even though the amount may be small but the same does not go unnoticed.

- For Instance, Karnataka Money Lending Statue[9] imposes restrictions against exorbitant interest rates.

The RBI guidelines even with the introduction of new norms of FPC and specific state statue have a limited oversight as these applies to DLPs linked with NBFCs and DLPs licensed form the state statue respectively.

Google Play Store- As a Regulator

As these pay day loan apps are accessible from Google Play stores making them responsible for hosting such apps. It has a Global Safety Policy[10] against lending app but the same is insufficient to regulate issues like exorbitant interest rates, harassment during recovery, misuse of personal data, etc.

As a result of these factors, a regulatory vacuum is created in which these DLPs operate unchecked and benefit from unsuspecting borrowers. Inadequate security for the user's personal data has led to use of harassment as a common practice[11].

<u>Chapter II- What is the impact and effectiveness of RBI issued norms ensuring strict and additional compliance with the Fair Practices Code and Outsourcing Guidelines?</u>

The RBI vide its notification[12], issued norms to ensure that the DLPs and the banks/ NBFCs strictly comply with the Fair Practices Code and Outsourcing Guidelines. This comes in light of various complaints received by RBI against such DLP. The main highlights of the notification are as follows:

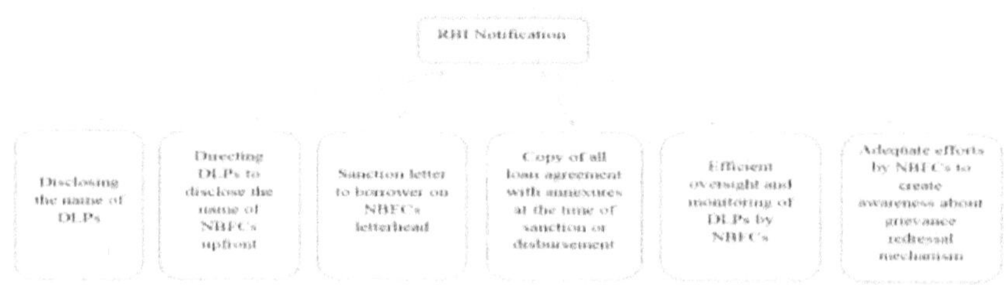

Impact on NBFCs and DLPs

The existing regulatory framework in terms of FPC contains a robust set of instructions. With the introduction of these norms RBI is trying to ensure to create an interface between the NBFC and the final consumer who are sourced through DLPs.[13] It is imperative to note that under these norms does not bring DLPs under the regulatory supervision of RBI as the same are intermediaries providing technology services. As per RBI the obligation of statutory compliance lies on NBFCs and Banks.[14] According to the author such stance is incorrect and some form of control over DLPs is a necessity. (The same will be discussed in Chapter III).

After the introduction of these additional norms NBFCs and Banks operating in digital lending segment may witness increased inspection in terms of their outsourcing agreement with DLPs and in some case may require changes including the need for providing grievance redressal mechanism system of NBFs and Banks to customers. DLPs will have to change their existing customer onboarding agreements to show upfront the name of the specific lender prior to the disbursement of the loan.[15]

Absence of Penal Actions

It is important to note that RBI has not specified any particular penal consequence in case the NBFCs or DLPs fails to comply with these norms. All it as mentioned is that violation will be taken up seriously.[16]

Regulatory Vacuum Still Exists

Even after the introduction of these measures the issues highlighted in Chapter I still exists to a large extent and a proposed resolution to the same will be provided in Chapter III.

<u>**Chapter III- What is the way forward?**</u>

The current judicial trend in terms of the petition filed, including the Save Them India Foundation petition[17] seeking a complete ban of these digital lending platforms and the recent Madras high court notice[18] to the state and center in a petition seeking a ban on the same matter, indicates a negative approach.

While the requests for a ban on fast lending applications are justified, the author argues that a total ban would be too harsh, as it would stifle the capital flow that the market need following the nationwide lockdown. A better way would be to regulate these applications by establishing a framework with which these apps would be forced to comply. The RBI has noticed this as well, and has formed a working committee (WG) for the same purpose.[19]

It is clear from the setting up of the WG that the light tough that was given by RBI to these DLPs may be facing a major overhaul. Whilst there is no doubt that a swift action is required to curb the malpractices followed by these DLPs but RBI and the WG should not tar the whole industry with the same brush imposing unnecessary strict regulations as it will act as a deterrent to the whole digital lending segment which has seen an increase foreign investment recently.

Keeping a balanced perspective of the risks involved and the growing digital lending segment including the protection of investors' interest , the RBI and WG should consider the following ideas and suggestions as a part of its terms of reference and while framing its final recommendations.

Avoid introduction of separate platform licensing- Introducing a new category of NBFC (like it did in the case of P2P lending) for DLPs will be an easy fix but the same would suffocate the industry, and digital innovation, which has always been the crucial aspect of India's Fintech revolution.

Introduction of Self-Regulatory Organization (SROs)- RBI is still finding its place as regulator in digital lending segment like most other Central banks around the globe. It can introduce a SRO for the segment which can ensure a healthy mix of regulatory and developmental needs of the industry. With RBI's backing it can act as board for policy decisions and as a enforcement agent of RBI.

Technology Standard and Consumer Data Protection- Technology is the base for Digital lening and the WG may prescribe baseline technology standards which can ensure security, data privacy and good governance. This will also ensure that those who can't keep up with the standard will be weeded out.

With regards to the Data protection, the author suggests that the same should be left with Personal Data Protection Bill and RBI imposing new norms in this regards will be uncalled for.

Consumer Grievance Redressal- In line with the existing Ombudsman scheme for Banks and NBFC, RBI can introduce a similar system for DLPs whilst the same can made eligible and authorized to deal with consumer grievance in this segment.

Holistic Approach- To encourage global investment and entry of big players in the market, the WG and RBI at a policy level should take a holistic approach. Hence, should refrain from imposing harsh restriction and ensure that some liberal approach is taken keeping in mind the 'Digital India' movement.[20]

However this problem is not limited to regulatory aspect alone but its lack of implementation too. The author propose that the Google Play store should ensure that those apps which are registered or linked with NBFCs or Banks and thus under the regulatory authority of RBI or apps that are licensed under state money lending statue should be allowed to be registered on its platform on a pre-screening basis. In this way the current vacuum can come to an end. Meanwhile the WG set up by RBI should create a holistic regulatory framework and also look into the feasibility of above-mentioned enforcement mechanism.

Conclusion

While these digital loan apps are undoubtedly a source of concern, it is crucial to highlight that these lending apps offer a lifeline for individuals who have been overlooked by our country's traditional credit system. By analyzing the problem caused by these apps and the policy vacuum that enabled such problems, this article identifies the lack of implementation of the existing frameworks, analyses the impact of new regulations and attempts to provide an enforcement mechanism that could help regulate the digital lending industry in an efficient manner with some suggestions for WC consideration while framing its final recommendations. The RBI, the state government, and platforms like Google and Apple must work in tandem to deal with the issue of unregulated digital lending apps